The 3 Habits of Highly Successful Reading Teachers

A QUICK AND EASY APPROACH TO HELPING ALL STUDENTS SUCCEED

Megan Milani

Pembroke Publishers Limited

Dedication
To all those who have persevered and overcome obstacles

© **2009 Pembroke Publishers**
538 Hood Road
Markham, Ontario, Canada L3R 3K9
www.pembrokepublishers.com

Distributed in the U.S. by Stenhouse Publishers
480 Congress Street
Portland, ME 04101
www.stenhouse.com

We acknowledge the financial support of the Government of Canada through the Book Publishing Industry Development Program (BPIDP) for our publishing activities.

We acknowledge the assistance of the Government of Ontario through the Ontario Media Development Corporation's Ontario Book Initiative.

Library and Archives Canada Cataloguing in Publication

Milani, Megan
    The 3 habits of highly successful reading teachers : a quick and easy approach to helping all students succeed / Megan Milani.

Includes bibliographical references and index.
ISBN 978-1-55138-239-5

    1. Reading (Primary). I. Title. II. Title: Three habits of highly successful reading teachers.

LB1573.M56 2009   372.4   C2009-902723-2

Editor: Kat Mototsune
Cover Design: John Zehethofer
Typesetting: Jay Tee Graphics Ltd.

Printed and bound in Canada
9 8 7 6 5 4 3 2 1

FSC
Mixed Sources
roduct group from well-managed
rests and other controlled sources

Cert no. SW-COC-002358
www.fsc.org
© 1996 Forest Stewardship Council

Contents

Introduction: Classrooms that Achieve Success in Reading

Learning to read is crucial. It is fundamental to everything we do. Learning to read is the first major academic event a student will encounter at school. Not only is reading an essential skill, the experience of learning to read has an enormous impact on future performance and confidence. When the experience is unsuccessful, students are often left believing that they are incapable. Their confidence is shattered and their motivation and drive disappears. They associate the difficulty they encounter when learning to read with all learning. When this happens to our students, true potential is not achieved and, as a society, we lose.

Through my work with struggling readers, I developed a successful reading program called LIFE — Literacy Is For Everyone. LIFE has been used as an intervention program and as part of the reading program for the early grades. *The 3 Habits of Highly Successful Reading Teachers* was born out of my experience with LIFE; it outlines how to implement the instruction and includes a new way of assessing students. It is my wish to share this with you, to help put an end to labels that limit and obstacles that prevent success.

In order to read, one needs to be able to decipher the code. Between 20% and 30% of our students struggle to do this. Too many read poorly or can barely read; these students lag farther and farther behind their peers. It is this group of students for which this book was written. When the 3 Habits are used, the number of students we fail can be reduced to zero.

What helps struggling students usually helps all students; the program has proven to accelerate the reading process for all children. Whether you teach Junior Kindergarten, where the reading process is just beginning, or Grade 8, where one of your students is unable or struggles to read, the 3 Habits will be a benefit to you.

What is the difference between classrooms that achieve success in reading and those where struggling readers are left behind? What do successful teachers do that really make students accelerate?

I have found that successful teachers have three important "habits" that underlie their reading instruction:

1. Successful teachers believe in their students.
2. Successful teachers teach and review high-frequency words (or sight words), letter sounds, and specific reading strategies on a daily basis.
3. Successful teachers assess their students. They know what their students need to learn. They regularly observe, record, and reflect on their findings.

Why do some students struggle to read? In my experience, these students struggle because they lack the visual memory required for most reading programs. But what if daily teaching focused on the child's auditory memory to teach reading? Students begin by using their auditory memory to remember letter sounds and high-frequency words. They are soon able to attend visually to these words. When you use the 3 Habits, the reading components are delivered in such a way as to make the process of retention possible. This, coupled with the explicit teaching of the reading strategies, ensures that every child is able to read independently.

The philosophy that runs throughout this book is the belief that everyone can learn to read. This book is for resource and classroom teachers. The habits are easy to learn and the reading components require only a few minutes each day.

1

Habit 1: Believing in Your Students

When I started as a remedial reading teacher, I knew there would be students in every class who would struggle with reading. I just thought that, if I worked hard with these kids on a one-on-one basis every day, they would all start to get it. Many students started to progress, but there were others who found learning to read so difficult that little or no progress was made, even with intensive support. Students like these are found in every school and in almost every classroom. It was this group of students that I kept wondering about.

One such student was Mary. She was not progressing well. I worked with this student every day. Despite my best efforts, she could not remember anything, not even a letter sound. Another teacher observed as I taught Mary and she agreed that Mary was not progressing, even though the delivery of the program was sound. I discussed Mary's lack of progress with her classroom teacher and with Mary's mother. We decided that the child was the problem and we removed Mary from the program. *Let's face it*, we thought, *if you are struggling to begin with, and then you struggle with the remedial reading teacher, there must be something wrong with you.* Mary was at the end of the road and she was only six years old.

The same thing happened with another child, and then another. If a child was not making the expected progress, that child was removed from the program.

My frustration eventually gave way to curiosity. How could these students struggle so much to remember letter sounds and words? I decided to step back and observe. Despite their lack of progress, these kids were capable in so many ways, so there had to be a way to reach them. What could they tell me about the way they learn? Finally, I found a way that worked. It begins with Habit 1 — believing in your students.

Paradigm Shift

"Whether you believe you can do a thing or not, you are right."
— Henry Ford

In order for reading instruction to be truly effective, a change in thinking may be required. We have to believe that every student in our classrooms can reach their full potential and will learn to read.

Often we determine that there is something wrong with a child who is not learning to read as well or as quickly as his or her peers — sometimes as early as when the child is six years of age. The way we judge students requires what is known as a paradigm shift. In *The 7 Habits of Highly Effective People* Stephen Covey discusses the need for a paradigm shift required to change ourselves for the better professionally and personally. Covey talks about Thomas Kuhn, who believed that every important breakthrough in science occurred because of a change in the way things were viewed. A paradigm shift may be what is needed in the classroom. We may have to observe our students through a new lens, and refrain from making judgments that put limits on kids. If we change the way we think, we will change the way we teach. If we truly believe that all children can learn to read, we will approach every child in a way that conveys our belief in him or her. We will have a true breakthrough if we change our thinking from "There is something wrong with the child" to "Perhaps there is something wrong with the way we are teaching or approaching the child."

Belief in your students is essential because, in order for students to thrive, they need to feel like they are capable. You need to believe to the core that your student can learn to read, and your student will start to believe it as well. We can all recall times when we were able to perform better because someone believed in us. When we believe that our students can learn to read, we are essentially setting the bar for success.

From day one of instruction, it is imperative that you tell each child that she or he is capable and is already making progress. I begin by saying that we are going to read together. We begin by chanting words (see page 16 in chapter 2). The child is quickly able to repeat the words that he or she hears. As soon as the child does this, I say "You are so smart! You already know these words!" This does wonders for the student, who is ecstatic at the teacher's praise. But the greatest thing is that the reading process has begun for this child. The struggling student will soon be able to retain high-frequency words and be set on the path to read at grade level.

Learning to read for some children is a tremendous feat. We have to remember that it is a lot of work, and that what may seem like a small step is really a huge leap. Celebrate every step taken toward the goal. Remember that your student will know how you feel because of what you say, the tone of your voice, and your body language. I find that it is the constant, genuine praise and the appreciation for what students have accomplished that is all that is necessary to keep them going. As students start to taste success, there is no stopping them!

Jacobson and Rosenthal (1968) studied the effect a teacher could have on students based on what the teacher's expectations were for those students. They went to a school and told the teacher that they were going to test her students. The researchers gave students an intelligence test, then chose 20% of the students at random and told the teacher that these students were the brightest and most likely to succeed. At the end of the year, these students were at the top of the class. The researchers concluded that the teacher subconsciously spent more time with these students, liked them more, and gave them more attention than the other children. They were expected to achieve, and they rose to the occasion.

Rosenthal and Jacobson's experiment confirmed that a teacher's expectations for students can serve as a self-fulfilling prophecy. We would not be human if we did not look at our students with subjectivity. However, if we were to look closely at even the simple things we subconsciously do each day, we would probably be stunned by the implications and the impact on our students. Rosenthal and Jacobson demonstrated that the teachers communicated to children through words and actions what they believed to be their true potential, and students in turn began to believe it about themselves.

We need to think about the messages we send, be it by tone, words, or body language. When we study student success and perceptions, patterns emerge. Children were able to read books at higher levels with teachers with whom they felt comfortable; i.e., teachers they felt liked them and thought they were smart. When asked how they knew the teacher felt that way, some students said they just knew, and others reported that their teachers often praised them and told

We all like to spend time on things that we are good at. If we believe in kids, tell them they are capable, students will want to spend the extra time becoming more proficient. Success breeds success.

them they were smart. Students reported that they liked reading with these teachers and said that the teacher smiled often (seemed happy) and seemed relaxed. How did the child know this? It seems like it was a combination of what the teacher said, the expression on the teacher's face, and the way the teacher interacted with the child.

The power that a teacher holds is extraordinary. A teacher can easily (and without realizing) alter a student's path in life for better or for worse. We all know teachers who changed people for the better. I can recall several students who were paid extra attention. Negative behaviors dissipated and attention to lessons improved. If you believe in a child, and that child knows that you do, the child will be successful.

Take the example of a student named David. David was often in trouble. Every time he was in trouble (and this was pretty often), he would be told by the principal that he was a good kid, regardless of the poor decisions he had made. One day, David arrived at the office and, after hearing about the infraction, the principal doled out a consequence. Then the principal said, "You're a good kid," and reminded David to make better decisions. David said, "That's what you keep telling me," and he smiled. It wasn't very long before David did start making better decisions and stopped getting into trouble. He had started to believe that he was a good kid.

Awareness

As humans, we are extremely adept at reading others. Our students have a good sense of what we think of them, if we believe in them, and what we expect of them. If we really believe that certain students are smart, we indicate this in the classroom. These students know that they are expected to do well. We spend time conversing with these students. Do we do the same for all students? If you really look closely at what you believe about your kids, and the things you do, surprising information will emerge. If you think your students do not know how you really feel, think again. We indicate our true feelings all the time. Expressions on our faces may be fleeting, but they are there and others are easily able to pick them up and ascertain what they mean. It is vital to know how much you can affect the students you teach and how well they do.

As educators, we certainly hope that we convey positive messages to our students. However, if we were to study our words and actions carefully, we would probably be shocked by the messages we send some of the time. Our messages often come from the subconscious part of our brains, and our awareness of these messages may be minimal.

Awareness is the first step. How do we become aware? Think about what you really believe and what your words and actions really say. Reflect on the words you use and the way you behave with your most struggling students. What internal dialog is going on? How are you feeling when you interact with the student? When I first started with struggling students, I was dismayed at how difficult reading was for some of them. I worked hard to help them remember one word, just to find that they couldn't recall the same word a minute later, and it left me feeling very frustrated. Although I did not intend it, I'm sure my body language and expression indicated that I had no faith in their ability.

Things won't change overnight, but if you believe — and I mean truly and deeply believe — that every child can learn to read, and you establish the habits

"Great teachers live in a world of vision. They are able to envision in their students what others cannot see. Because they can see greatness in their students, they are able to build greatness in their students." (Richardson, 2009)

of successful reading instruction, then that will become the reality. What you convey will directly affect your students and ensure that the child believes in himself or herself. Try recording your thoughts, feelings, and observations in a journal to help you understand what you are feeling and, thus, what you are conveying. Another good idea is to use a mirror. Close your eyes and visualize yourself teaching a struggling student. Remember how you felt. Imagine that you are teaching the child now. Look in the mirror and study your expression. I've tried this, and what I saw in the mirror surprised me. I was taken aback by what my facial expressions revealed. We often think that we are able to mask our feelings. In *Blink*, Malcolm Gladwell describes how we often are surprised when somebody reads our expression. Gladwell states that "if we knew what was on our face, we would be better at concealing it." (2005: 210) Try the mirror; take note of what you see.

Changing the Messages

Once we are aware of what we are conveying to our students, we can then make any necessary changes. Change can be difficult. It is not that we don't want to change; it's that we often don't realize there's a need for change or how to go about making the change.

Kegan and Lahey (2001: 70) discuss the big assumptions we hold to be true with absolute certainty, to the point where we don't think "to look for a different reality." The authors tell the story of an Australian woman living in the US who was having a hard time getting used to driving on "the wrong side" of the road. One day she got in the car, only to find the steering wheel was not in front of her. "My God," she thought, "here in the United States things have gotten so bad, they are even stealing steering wheels!" As humorous as it is, Kegan and Lahey note that the truth was just "an arm's length to her left." We don't think to look for the truth if we are certain we already know it.

We can apply this thinking to the assumptions we hold about our students: if we believe that a student is not capable, we essentially open the wrong door of the car and go nowhere. If we don't believe our students can learn, why would we teach them? Perhaps we need to begin by bringing our big assumptions down to where we can at least challenge them — as assumptions "whose truth status is uncertain." (Kegan and Lahey, 2001)

How do we buy into change? Most professional books and articles about change view change as an unwelcome beast that does not happen without much pain and work, and this is usually the case. It is often believed that we change by first "buying in" to the idea, and then our actions will change. My experience has led me to believe that if we change our actions and have positive experiences, the end result is the "buy in."

In order to change our actions we need to attend to our internal dialog. Pause and listen to your thoughts. Choose to stop the negative thoughts of what a child can't do and change them to a positive view of what the child can do. Do this several times a day. Then, focus on your external dialog, what you say to your kids. Record the words you use to encourage your struggling readers. When you start to implement the 3 Habits, you might choose to use the script that you will find in this book. We have to convey, at least by our words, that we believe in all of our kids. The script uses positive words and phrases. Use of the script will ensure that you are reiterating what the child *can* do and that the language is always positive. Saying "No, that was wrong, try that again," is much different from, "You know that word. Here it is. Let's read from here." When we take away the negatives and make an effort to change what we say, the impact is huge.

When we consciously change what we say, our body language will start to change with it. Our expressions will start to mimic the message we send orally. When you see a teacher conversing with students, you hear the positive message in the oral remarks. If you're not within earshot, it is still obvious that that the teacher is thinking positively about the child. The teacher's expression and posture convey what he or she is feeling.

When we see the changes in our students due to the positive messages they are receiving, and witness the progress they start to make, our belief in their ability will begin to change as well. It is difficult to believe in all of our kids all of the time, as the learning can at times be slow and laborious, but it is important to make the effort even when it's hard. Similarly, parents can find it difficult to be positive all the time. As a parent, it is easy to think of the times you helped your child with homework and when, despite your best effort and time spent, your child just wasn't getting it. The frustration you felt was tremendous! Being aware of how we're feeling and what message we are sending is the first step. In the end, we all come to the same conclusion. Our kids are capable — sometimes we just have to teach in a different way.

Looking through a New Lens

When I present the 3 Habits to teachers, there is sometimes skepticism. But, despite reservations, these teachers start to look at reading with a new lens. What is there to lose? They have students for whom conventional programs have proven ineffective so they give it a try.

Feelings of skepticism are normal. It takes time to believe that all students can be successful. As you start to work with your students, and see the success, you will start to change your thinking and marvel at how capable your students really are.

The LIFE program, on which the 3 Habits are based, has been used by classroom and resource teachers with great success from Junior Kindergarten to Grade 8. The program has also been successful with second-language learners, and students identified with exceptionalities and speech delays. Most students begin to read well beyond grade level. All students, struggling or not, tend to learn to read at a much quicker pace than when using other programs.

Besides asking teachers to look at reading in a new way, we discuss the importance of looking at students in a new way. We have to believe all students can learn to read. It's well known that physical development in children occurs at varying rates and ages. Puberty can begin as early as nine in some and almost twice that age in others. This whole range is considered normal. Would it not seem likely or normal that children could also have different rates in their mental development? If a child's visual memory wasn't as easily stimulated as another's, should we say that child can't learn? Should we just lessen the load and lower the bar? Perhaps it is not that there is something wrong with the child. Perhaps it is the way we approach the child.

What about children with memory problems? Does the program work for them? In my experience, if a child can communicate verbally, he or she certainly has the mental capacity required to read. Take the example of computer processing: software is available that allows computers to read text. This technology has been available for some time. Although the voice may sound unnatural, there is no doubt that a computer can perform this skill. On the other hand, developing software so that computers can converse (not just talk) is a major hurdle in computer science that is currently being tackled by some of the greatest minds in the field. Reading is a simpler task than communicating.

When a child struggles to learn to read, it is often thought that the child lacks the ability to read. I have found that this could not be further from the truth. Some children lag behind in the reading process due to many factors, such as lack of motivation, confidence, and visual memory — but certainly not because of a lack of ability. Regardless of the complicating factors, it is our responsibility to provide them with the skills to ensure they succeed.

Some teachers wonder about students who have been diagnosed with multiple problems. Some have been identified as being learning disabled; some are hard to understand because of their speech problems. How do they fare? What about discipline issues? We teach the program to all kids who are reading below grade level, regardless of diagnoses and problems.

It doesn't matter where your students are from or how much income the family earns — all students can learn to read. Reading has to be treated as the single most important thing to master. If not, the child will be set up for a life of failure. Changing the at-risk student statistics begins with reading success. A child won't be able to do anything in school if he or she cannot read. What the child will do at school is misbehave.

Students start to feel successful from the start and disruptive behaviors drop dramatically. Students feel good about themselves. All students will jump several reading levels, and most will read at grade level in a very short period of time, regardless of the diagnoses and problems. For many students who struggle with reading, this is the first time they experience any academic success at school.

Habit 2: The Reading Components

2

In my work developing the 3 Habits, I kept asking myself: how could students have so much trouble remembering letters and words when they could engage in conversation, rhyme off all kinds of games, remember their favorite movies, and recount events from the day before? I started to tutor students (I canvassed for struggling students in the neighborhood) and tried all kinds of things to get them to remember the letter sounds and high-frequency words. After much trial and error, I found that some methods helped a bit but nothing made much difference. They just couldn't remember the words, no matter how many times we reviewed and read the books. It seemed their visual memory just wasn't there yet.

I started to observe the students carefully and to make notes. There are certain things that struggling readers have in common. They do not know, or often confuse, the letter sounds. They do not recognize the high-frequency words. These kids might recognize a word like "look" on one page, and then will not recognize it on the next. Struggling readers do not know what to do when they are stuck on a word. What they learn is to do one of two things: they freeze or guess. Struggling students find that these two strategies have worked really well for them because, in the end, we provide the word to them!

There had to be a way for these kids to remember the letter sounds and high-frequency words. They needed to learn useful strategies (not freezing and guessing) in order to read other words they encounter.

I thought back to how my daughter learned to read many years ago. I started thinking about the sight-word lists that were sent home. I brought out the Dolch word list, and introduced the Dolch words to the students I was tutoring. I soon found that they were able to repeat the words on the list, even though they did not attend much to the visual characteristics of the words. Every day I would start at the top of the list, pointing to each word; I would add a word a day. The students were essentially chanting the words; I didn't realize at this point that the chanting was absolutely necessary. All I knew was that these kids were capable, and somehow or other they needed to learn these words.

The students would chant away, and I would constantly praise them and tell them how great it was that they knew so many words. The truth was, they weren't able to read any of these words. But they certainly could rhyme them off with no problem. Before long, the students could recite the first 40 words on the list. Here I was with students who could recite a lot of words, but still couldn't read any books! But soon, this chanting of the words enabled my students to recognize the words. For the first time, these struggling readers had a bank of high-frequency words.

I used the chanting method to help students remember letter sounds too. To understand how the chanting works, think of the alphabet song and how we would sing it as students everyday in school. We would look at the letters and

"If we wait long enough, either the teacher will give us the answer or the period will be over."— A high-school student's reply to why she doesn't answer questions (Slavin, Holmes, Daniels, 2008)

sing away. The singing, just like chanting, helps us remember. When it is done to the point of memorization, the letters (or words, in the case of the Dolch list) become a frame of reference. We begin by saying (or singing) the letters; then we look at the letters in order. At first, we are able to say the letters only by using the song, but eventually we can recall them without this aid. For struggling students, the chanting is critical and enables them to retain the words with ease. If you don't believe that having a frame of reference is important, try to say the letters of the alphabet randomly and see how well you do. Try typing on a keyboard with the letters randomly placed. We use frames of reference all the time.

Several staff members bought into the idea and worked with older students who were lagging behind. All students improved; most accelerated quickly and started reading grade-level text and beyond. The first school that I brought the 3 Habits to was in a low socio-economic area and many students struggled to read. To change this reality, intervention and preventive action was required. Students needed instruction that would help them catch up to their peers, and those starting school needed it before the reading problems started. I was teaching Junior Kindergarten and I used my new method to teach my students to read. Some students were learning English as a second language and some had speech delays, but not one lacked enthusiasm.

I began with my Junior Kindergarten students in the same way as I did with the students I had tutored — by teaching the high-frequency words. These young students began, as you can imagine, by not looking at the words at all and just repeating them. But that was okay — I just needed them to memorize the words at this point. Every day we went over the words in the same order. When they had mastered repeating the words, I added another. We had a great time memorizing the list. They would shout it out, jump it out, and dance it out. While waiting outside to be picked up by parents at the end of the day, they would start chanting the words together as a group and the parents would won-der what was going on!

I told my students constantly how well they were learning to read. I sent the word list and books home with my students, and showed the parents how to teach them. Soon, the parents were requesting more books to be sent home. Everyone was telling these students they were smart.

The results for these Junior Kindergarten students were excellent. Many students were reading well above grade level. We had to borrow books from the other primary classes, as the books I had in my Junior Kindergarten class were too easy. One boy started reading at a Grade 5 level.

I worked every day with students who were not progressing as fast as their peers. This only required a few minutes a day. The bar was set very high, and everyone was rising to the occasion. It worked well not only for students who would have found learning to read difficult — it also advanced the reading process for all my other students.

Habit 2 involves teaching three reading components on a daily basis: high-frequency words, letter sounds, and reading strategies. Teaching the three components requires only a few minutes each day.

High-Frequency Words

Materials Needed:
- the Power Words list (pages 20–21)
- chart of words from the column you will be using (see pages 22–26)
- duotangs for small-group and individual work
- approximately two minutes a day for whole-class work

Anthropologists have long known that prior to the written word, humans passed important information to their children through song (similar to chanting). The children were able to remember information vital to their survival, such as knowing which plants are poisonous, and how to be safe. Our ancestors knew that if words were set to a rhythm, they were easier to retain.

Since the Dolch list was compiled, many sight word lists have been created. But the words are much the same. The chanting method would work with any word list, but I like the order of the words as shown on pages 20–21; and they lend themselves well to rhythmic chanting.

In order to read, students need to be able to read high-frequency words, in isolation and embedded in text, quickly and with ease. The easiest way to teach any child (struggling or not) to learn the high-frequency words is to tap into their ability to chant.

The Dolch list of high-frequency words was compiled by Edward William Dolch in 1948. The 220 words on this list make up 50% to 75% of all the words that we read. These words are referred to as the high-frequency or sight words.

It is imperative that students learn these words by sight — as pictures. High-frequency words are not to be broken down and sounded out. Students need to be able to instantly recognize and read these words by sight.

To chant the words, the class says the words in unison in a rhythmic way. You will chant the word list each day with your whole class, while pointing at each word as it is chanted. The chanting of the high-frequency words is important because the students are empowered when they are able to "read" words. Thus, the couple of minutes it takes to chant the words is necessary. For some students who have struggled for quite some time, the belief that they are actually reading will fuel the fire to learn more. They feel like readers from the first day you begin the program.

The chanting approach is the only method I have found to help these students retain the high-frequency words. It seems to me that the auditory memory helps to stimulate the visual memory. It starts with the chanting. At the same time, they are looking at the words as you point. Eventually, the child starts to pick up some visual information and retain it. Recognizing the words without the aid of the chant will come later. You will help them transfer these words to text (see page 32). Soon they will be able to recognize the words without using the chant.

The column you use is determined by a diagnostic assessment (see pages 53–56). Of your struggling readers, the one that scores the lowest on the diagnostic determines which column of the list you will display and chant in your classroom. Even if you are teaching Grade 3, and the student with the lowest reading level is working on the Level 1 column, this is the list you use for the class. The teaching and reviewing of the list is always geared toward the lowest-level reader in the class.

The class should not know that chanting the high-frequency words is to help certain students. One of the biggest secrets of the 3 Habits is that struggling readers feel smart. For a couple of minutes a day, they are doing what everyone else is doing. They don't know that what the class is doing is really for them. Perhaps, for the first time in their school life, struggling readers feel normal in the classroom. Our job as educators is to provide opportunities for success.

At one school starting to implement the 3 Habits, a student in their special-needs class was autistic and nonverbal, and would not attend at all when the class was chanting. Eventually, he started looking at the words on the chart paper. One day, he jumped up when the class started to chant, took the pointer, and started pointing at the words. Soon after, he pointed and started to say the words. The lesson to me, and to the elated teacher and staff at this school, was to not put limitations on our kids. My experience to that point was that if a child can converse, he can learn to read. This particular child challenged that assumption.

Why chant the list with the whole class if only a few kids need it? The minute or two that it takes will do wonders for your struggling kids and will not hurt the others. I have found that students enjoy chanting the list as a class. Chanting has been used therapeutically to calm children and I often observe them rocking back and forth as they recite the words. As I observe classes chanting the high-frequency words, I can tell that even students who are reading well above level are enjoying it. When I visit classrooms, the kids often want to show me how well they can chant the list. Students who can already read these words may benefit from the chanting, as the activity might help them with spelling and patterns.

Starting the Chanting

Teaching and reviewing the high-frequency words starts with displaying and chanting one column of the Power Words list (see pages 20–21).

- Begin by saying, "We are going to read some words together." Be sure to refer to the activity as "reading" and not "chanting." Many of the students in your class may know the words already and one might say, "I know all these words." You'll just reply, "That's great. We're going to read them together every day."

- Start with the first word: if your class is starting with the Level 1 list, say, "a" while pointing to the word. Repeat the word three times with your students. Then have your students as a group say the word independently of you while you point at the word on the chart.

- The next day, add one word — "a, and" — and have your students chant with you, saying the words three times. Then you say, "Now you say it." The class will chant the words independently of you. The goal is to have all the words in the column memorized in order.

- The next day, do the same thing and add one word — "a, and, away." Your students chant with you, saying these three words three times. Then you say, "Now you say it." While you point to the chart paper, your students say "a, and, away."

- Continue reviewing the list from the top and adding one word per day, whether or not all students can keep up that pace. Hearing the list and watching you point to the words is all that it will take to get your most struggling student remembering these words.

- Your students will be memorizing the words at the beginning. They will want to show you how they can say the words without looking. Listen to them, praise them, and then say "That's great. We're going to look at the words, too, as we say them."

Never suggest to the child that the words are being memorized. You must be sure that everyone helping the child to read knows ahead of time that we never say, "You just have it memorized." Instead we always say, "You can read a lot of words."

> **Tips for Chanting High-Frequency Words**
>
> - Together, speak the words with much enthusiasm, almost as though you are cheering.
> - Do not make the chant into a song. This will impede the child's ability to recognize the word when it's embedded in text.
> - While singing is discouraged, I certainly suggest dancing, snapping fingers, clapping, jumping if you need to liven things up!
> - Never test your students by mixing up the sight words. Observe, encourage, and support by bringing students back to the chanting — something that is safe and familiar, and that helps them remember. (Assessment is discussed in chapter 3.)
> - Always point to each word as it is chanted.
> - Some teachers call upon student volunteers to point to the words for the class to chant. Some teachers provide a magic wand for students to point. As your struggling readers get good at the chanting, call them up to lead the class.
> - Encourage all students to be looking at the words.
> - Add only one word a day.
> - Whenever you can plan or steal a minute, have a struggling student review the words again. Keep the Power Words list at hand in a duotang for one-on-one or small-group work (see page 18).
> - Be patient and praise your students and they will be successful.

If a student is not progressing as quickly as you hoped, the child is not failing; the learning process is just taking a little longer. Your job is to persist. "If most of the class doesn't get it, it is our responsibility. If 25 percent of the class doesn't get it, it is still our responsibility. And if one child doesn't get it, it remains our responsibility" (Harvey and Goudvis, 2007: 39).

You will notice that some of your struggling students will not be attending visually at all. Some may not be saying the words. Encourage them to look, but it may take time for some of them to focus and join in. This is fine, as the goal is to have the chant memorized. Being able to recognize the words will come later. Students who are less focused will hear the other kids saying the words, and will memorize the chant that way. They will eventually join in because it is easy for them and they feel successful; soon they will be looking at the words too.

When chanting with the whole class, the struggling student will go as far as he or she can, and the class will continue as you add one word per day. At some point, perhaps after 15 words (15 days), the struggling student might mouth the words or echo the words he or she hears. This is to be expected and this is progress. We still say that all students can read all those words and we do not "notice" that one is pretending to chant. The student is still attending and hears the words in order every day.

The high-frequency words should be so well memorized that the students can rhyme them off without looking at the words (but of course we want them looking too!). What is crucial here is the use of the auditory memory. We want the child to be able to remember the words in order by hearing the chant.

It is imperative that the list be chanted in the way described here. Resist the urge to mix up the words or put the list words on flashcards. You will probably think to yourself, *the child is just memorizing them but can't read them* — and you'll be right. This is what we want. Remember that struggling students find it very hard to retain high-frequency words, so isolating the words will not help them.

Never test your students by taking the words out of order. The 3 Habits are about empowering and making students feel like readers from the very first lesson. If you test the child and he or she doesn't do well, that student will not feel empowered and will not feel like a reader. Assessment of how well your students are doing is discussed starting on page 41. Always set up the child for success. Praise the child for every small step gained, and always make the chanting of the words interesting and fun by being enthusiastic and energetic.

Adding Columns

As a class, you've been adding one word per day. Every day, the words are chanted. You have reached the end of that column. Now what? Keep chanting the words on that column until they are completely mastered by all your students; i.e., every child in the class can chant the words without hesitation.

The first column you do with your class takes the longest to memorize. That is because the students are getting accustomed to the chanting, the memorization process, and attending to the words on some level. It may take a couple of months, if not longer (depending on students and grade) to memorize the first column. Just be patient and it will come.

When I refer to mastering, it does not mean that all students can actually read the words. Mastering means that the child has the list memorized, in order, and can say the words without hesitation.

- Once the column is mastered (memorized), move on to the next column and start the same way, with the first word. Say it three times with your kids, then have your students together say the word independently of you.

- Add one word a day. You can keep the old list up and chant that quickly, too, when class time permits.

- The student at the lowest reading level always determines which list you work on as a class; for example, don't go to the Level 2 column if every student hasn't memorized Level 1.

Imagine your class has mastered Level 1 and has just started the Level 2 column; it's January and you get a new student. Stay at Level 2 but chant the Level 1 list too. You don't want to frustrate the class by moving back. Work one-on-one with the new student to get that student caught up to the rest of the class. In other words, it's important to not go ahead when the student furthest behind is not ready, but if you get a new student and your class has worked hard to move to the next column, don't go back.

Small-Group and Individual Work

Once you get other students engaged in their learning during the literacy block, it is easy to take a minute to go over the chanting of high-frequency words again with just the small group that needs it. The effort is minimal and the payoff is huge. Every day I would schedule my students who were reading below grade level for a session that would take only a couple of minutes.

Imagine you have three students who are working below grade level in your class. They are working to memorize the first column of the high-frequency words, Level 1. The whole class will chant the words starting with *a* and then you will add one word a day. Your three struggling readers may or may not appear to keep up at this pace, but the adding of one word a day is the pace you work at with the whole class.

Teachers of Grade 3 and up are encouraged to work one-on-one with students who are below grade level, as students at this age may feel embarrassed at their lack of word knowledge. Details about teaching older students are found in chapter 5.

- Work with this group every day (ideally, during your scheduled guided reading time; see chapter 3).

- Copy the whole Power Words list (pages 20–21) (all 5 columns) and put it in a reading duotang for each student working below level.

- When you work with them as a small group, go at their pace. Have them chant down as far as they can (until the last voice dies out). Then add one word, and say all the words to that point with them again three times.

- Go to the top of the column again and tell them it is their turn.

- If your students cannot remember the new word, repeat it again. Do not ask the student to sound out the word; give the student the word immediately.

- Go to the top of the column they are working on and start chanting again together; chant a total of three times.

- Have the students point to the words. If a student is unable to do the one-to-one match, take his or her finger and point for the student. It should take one second to say and point to each word.

- When working with students on a one-on-one basis, have the students point and recite the words as far as they can without assistance. When a student is stuck, give the word and start again, saying the list to that point three times together. Then ask the student to say the words with the new word added.

Having the students point to the words themselves is important. The one-to-one match means that the child points to each word as he or she says it. We want to provide every opportunity possible for students to do things on their own on the road to independence. Pointing will also encourage students to look while they are chanting, and will prevent them from saying the words too quickly — as they get good at memorizing the words, they sometimes race through them and they cannot attend visually at that speed.

Make copies of the Power Words list (pages 20–21) and have all students who are not at grade level keep them in a duotang in their desks. Because the students are successful from the start, they like to work at it. Having the list handy will encourage the student to practice. They don't seem to worry — or even notice — that some students don't have a duotang, if you provide the list discreetly. I have watched students pull their duotang out and chant the words to themselves when they have a minute to spare. These are students that were previously unmotivated, had no interest in school, and were always off-task. They love the success they are experiencing and want to keep working at it.

It is highly recommended that students chant the list words several times a day. For example, students can chant the words with the class and then with you during guided reading. They can chant later in the day with a volunteer, and then with a parent at night. If a child needs to see the list several times in order to be successful, then provide the child with this. The more often the child chants the list and points to the words, the quicker he or she will learn to read. The more often, the better — just not all in one sitting! Chanting the list words for more than a couple of minutes at one sitting is tedious; break it up with the other components of the program (i.e., letter sounds, reading strategies), and then go back and chant the list again.

Students who are not at grade level need you to work with them each day as they obviously need the most assistance. Students working at grade level will receive the next level of assistance, and students working above grade level will work with you probably just once per week.

Power Words, Part 1

Level 1	Level 2	Level 3	Level 4	Level 5
a	all	after	always	about
and	am	again	around	better
away	are	an	because	bring
big	at	any	been	carry
blue	ate	as	before	clean
can	be	ask	best	cut
come	black	by	both	done
down	brown	could	buy	draw
find	but	every	call	drink
for	came	fly	cold	eight
funny	did	from	does	fall
go	do	give	don't	far
help	eat	going	fast	full
here	four	had	first	got
I	get	has	five	grow
in	good	her	found	hold
is	has	him	gave	hot
it	he	how	goes	hurt
jump	into	just	green	if
little	like	know	its	keep
look	must	let	made	kind
make	new	live	many	laugh
me	no	may	off	light
my	now	of	or	long
not	on	old	pull	much
one	our	once	read	myself

Power Words, Part 2

Level 1	Level 2	Level 3	Level 4	Level 5
play	out	open	right	never
red	please	over	sing	only
run	pretty	put	sit	own
said	ran	round	sleep	pick
see	ride	some	tell	seven
the	saw	stop	their	shout
three	say	take	these	show
to	she	thank	those	six
two	so	them	upon	small
up	soon	then	us	start
we	that	think	use	ten
yellow	there	walk	very	today
you	they	where	wash	together
	this	when	which	try
	too		why	were
	under		wish	
	want		work	
	was		would	
	well		write	
	went		your	
	what			
	white			
	who			
	will			
	with			
	yes			

Adapted from Dolch (1948)

Power Words: Level 1

a	look
and	make
away	me
big	my
blue	not
can	one
come	play
down	red
find	run
for	said
funny	see
go	the
help	three
here	to
I	two
in	up
is	we
it	yellow
jump	you
little	

Power Words: Level 2

all	out
am	please
are	pretty
at	ran
ate	ride
be	saw
black	say
brown	she
but	so
came	soon
did	that
do	there
eat	they
four	this
get	too
good	under
has	want
he	was
into	well
like	went
must	what
new	white
no	who
now	will
on	with
our	yes

Power Words: Level 3

after	let
again	live
an	may
any	of
as	old
ask	once
by	open
could	over
every	put
fly	round
from	some
give	stop
going	take
had	thank
has	them
her	then
him	think
how	walk
just	where
know	when

Power Words: Level 4

always	or
around	pull
because	read
been	right
before	sing
best	sit
both	sleep
buy	tell
call	their
cold	these
does	those
don't	upon
fast	us
first	use
five	very
found	wash
gave	which
goes	why
green	wish
its	work
made	would
many	write
off	your

Power Words: Level 5

about	laugh
better	light
bring	long
carry	much
clean	myself
cut	never
done	only
draw	own
drink	pick
eight	seven
fall	shout
far	show
full	six
got	small
grow	start
hold	ten
hot	today
hurt	together
if	try
keep	were
kind	

Letter Sounds

Materials Needed:
- Letter Sounds sheet (see page 30)
- individual letter cards copied and enlarged from the Letter Sounds sheet
- reading duotangs for small-group and individual work
- approximately one minute per day

Like the chanting of the high-frequency words, chanting the letter sounds takes a minute or so each day, and can be done with the whole class or in small groups. Until every student has the individual letter sounds and combinations mastered, the 3 Habits include a daily letter-sound component.

From your diagnostic assessment (see pages 53–56), you know which students need practice with the individual letter sounds and which ones do not. You may have a student who cannot read at a very high level but knows all the individual letter sounds; there is no need to work on the letter sounds with this type of student, but it would be time to do a diagnostic assessment on letter combinations.

> ### The Rule of 5
>
> - If you have more than five students who do not know the letter sounds, review the sounds every day with the whole class for just a minute.
> - If you have five or fewer students who still need to master the letter sounds, this can be done with daily small-group work.

Use your own set of letter cards if you wish. When the 3 Habits are used schoolwide, it is preferable to have all students, volunteers, and teachers using the same set.

Why is five the magic number for deciding on whole-class or small-group work? A group of more than five students is not as manageable; it is easier to address the letter sounds with the whole class. Since it takes only a minute, the students who already know the letter sounds will not have their learning impeded. As with anything you implement, you will use your professional judgment in deciding if whole-class instruction will have a negative effect on your students emotionally. If your students who are below level in reading are at an age where whole-class instruction would highlight their situation, small-group work may be more effective.

Introducing Individual Letter Sounds

Work with the entire class to teach letter sounds if more than five students require it. There is no need to discuss the letter name, just the letter sound; reading is not about naming letters, it is about knowing the sounds. The letter names will be taught incidentally in other parts of your comprehensive literacy block; i.e., when you are doing writing activities you will talk about letter names and point them out, print them, spell them, etc. If we are going to get our students reading, we need to concentrate on the sounds the letters make.

- Begin by posting an enlarged *A a — apple* card on the board.

- Point to the uppercase and lowercase letters as you say, "A, a." Remember to make the letter sound, not name the letter.

- Say, "apple," while pointing to the apple.

- Have your students repeat it with you three times: "A, a, apple."

- Ask your students to repeat it together.

- The next day, move on to the next sound. Post the A card and the B card. Say "A, a, apple," and "B, b, bat." Chant the letters in order three times. Have the students say it independently.

- Review the taught letter sounds and add one letter sound each day.

Tips for Chanting Letter Sounds and Combinations

- Together, speak the sounds and words with much enthusiasm, almost as though you are cheering.
- When reading the card, make the sound of the letter. Do not name the letter.
- Always point to each letter and picture as it is chanted.
- Chant the letters in order and keep them posted in order in your classroom. This is a process of memorization and establishing a frame of reference.
- Focus on the child who is farthest behind. If you have extra time, give it to that student. Most of your students will accelerate quickly; you will be tempted to forge on and get them even further ahead — but those students will be fine. You have to ensure that *all* your kids will be successful, so don't give up on the one who needs you the most.
- Be patient and praise your students and they will be successful.

Small-Group and Individual Work

The chanting of all the letter sounds is necessary if there are several letter sounds the child does not know. If you have a child who confuses only the vowel sounds, have this student chant only these sounds. Remember to concentrate on the short vowel sounds and the hard *G* and *C*. The long vowel sounds and soft *G* and *C* will be taught incidentally in other areas of your literacy program.

If you're delivering this component to a small group (five or fewer students) rather than the whole class, you will use the Letter Sounds sheet (page 30). Photocopy the sheet and place the copies in their reading duotangs. Keep a copy for yourself.

By working with your students daily, you'll know how their needs change as they progress through the program. Are they unsure of vowel sounds? Are some in need of help with all sounds?

If one student in the group needs a good review of all the sounds, it will likely be a good review for all students in the group. Since it takes only a minute, it will not adversely affect anyone in the group.

- Start at the beginning with "A, a, apple." Point to the letters and pictures on your copy of the Letter Sheet.

- Have the group take part, pointing to the letters and pictures on their Letter Sheets. Chant the sounds together three times and ask the students as a group to repeat "A, a, apple."

- The next day, review "A, a, apple." Add the next letter: "B, b, bat."

- Chant "A, a, apple; B, b, bat" together three times, then ask the students to repeat it as a group.

- Follow the pattern and add one letter a day.

You will know when a student has mastered the individual letter sounds by listening to the student read. You will hear the student say the sound of letters and sound out words as he or she starts to learn the reading strategies. When you are confident that a student knows the sounds, go back to diagnostic testing (see page 56) for individual letter sounds and see how the student does. Perhaps there are only a couple of letter sounds that will need daily review. Just review those sounds and soon your student will be ready for the combinations.

Letter Combinations

Materials Needed:
- Combinations sheet (see page 31)
- individual letter-combinations cards copied and enlarged from the Combinations sheet
- reading duotangs
- approximately one minute per day

Once students solidly know the individual letter sounds, complete the diagnostic for the combinations (see page 56). Again, your professional judgment is needed to determine how to proceed with delivering the combinations. In Grade 1, the entire class would probably benefit from reviewing the digraphs and blends on the Combinations. Most Grade 3 students would probably know these sounds. Use the Rule of 5 to help you determine the most efficient way to deliver this component.

For whole-class teaching, use cards copied and enlarged from the Combinations sheet. For small-group or individual teaching, use the Combinations sheet (page 30); photocopy the Combinations sheet and have students place a copy in their reading duotangs.

- Use the letter-combinations cards or Combinations sheet to teach and review digraphs and blends. Introduce the combinations by saying, "These letters stay together when you see them."

- Start with the *sh* —*she* combination. Say, "We keep *s* and *h* together and they say 'sh' — like in the word 'she'."

- Go over the other combinations and give the example under the sound.

- The next day, the chanting will start. Concentrate on the sounds; omit the examples. Point to the first combination and say "sh." Chant the same way as you would the words and letter sounds — three times together

- Add one sound a day.

When working one-on-one, you may notice that your student says the sound incorrectly. Have the student watch you, and describe how you make the sound. For example, for *th*, say, "Look at me. When we make this sound, stick your tongue out, like this." It may be helpful to use a mirror so students can see where to place their own tongues.

Students with speech delays may not say all sounds correctly. After modeling and using the mirror, accept the sound as they say it. They will continue to hear it from you and they will know the sound, even if they are not producing it correctly. Chances are that the child is receiving help with his or her speech; discuss it with the child's speech pathologist, who may be able to offer suggestions.

Letter Sounds

Combinations

<u>sh</u> she	<u>th</u> the	<u>ch</u> chip
<u>er</u> her	<u>ir</u> girl	<u>ar</u> car
<u>ou</u> out	<u>ow</u> now	<u>ow</u> snow
<u>ea</u> eat	<u>ee</u> see	<u>ay</u> day
<u>ew</u> new	<u>oy</u> boy	<u>oi</u> join
<u>oo</u> soon	<u>ur</u> turn	<u>oa</u> coat

Transfer of Words

The Transfer of Words and Reading Strategies components are delivered to small groups or one-on-one if numbers allow. Some teachers find extra time in the day in addition to the guided-reading time. They schedule small-group or individual work while other students are reading silently. Reading with your students can be done a couple of times per day or once during the guided-reading time. It can be as quick as a couple of minutes per student (usually covering a couple of pages), or as long as 10 to 15 minutes. Reading books with your students brings all the subskills together, builds fluency, exposes students to an endless bank of words, shows them the rules of the English language at work, and, most of all, fosters a great love of reading and pride in what they've accomplished. Any time you read books with your students, whether it's in guided-reading groups or one-on-one instruction, the transfer of words and reading strategies take place.

What is the point of small-group instruction? If all your students were working at the same level, there would be little need for small groupings. Your small-group sessions are based on the information you gain from assessing students, and provide you with a chance to differentiate instruction, to provide support and learn more about your students — their strengths and areas for growth. Reading is about deciphering text with ease (decoding) and extracting deep understanding of text. Students working below grade level in their decoding skills will need you to work with them every day to improve.

In your small group, review the high-frequency words and the letter sounds by chanting. Select a book at the appropriate instructional level to transfer the words and teach reading strategies. It only requires a few minutes of your guided reading session, but the instruction is powerful and ensures that these sight words are learned solidly. Then you can move on to the rest of your guided reading lesson involving instruction for deep understanding of text.

Students who are reading below level need to be placed in a guided-reading group to work on decoding every day. Small groups are feasible and work well, but individual instruction is even better. If you have only a couple of students who are struggling, you may be able to work with them on a one-on-one basis. As part of the diagnostic assessment you will complete an Observation Record (see pages 53–55) for each student, so you can easily determine the level at which that student can read. Students in one group may have a range of reading levels. You may have some reading at level 6 and some at level 8 in one group. You will want to group students who are as close to the same level as possible.

Students may be able to chant the words in a list, but how will this help them read? The same day you begin chanting the high-frequency words, start helping your students transfer these words to text using guided reading.

When I worked as a remedial reading teacher, struggling readers commonly could not keep the high-frequency words straight. If they couldn't nail the high-frequency words, it was too laborious to even start tackling the other words. Their fluency was greatly impeded, and so the meaning was not always carried well.

Once your struggling reader is able to recognize the high-frequency words in the text, he or she will be able to tackle the other words. The quick recognition of the high-frequency words will enable greater fluency, so meaning will not be lost. The only way that I've found to get these students to remember the words is by starting with the chanting, and then helping them transfer the words to the text they are reading.

Learning the words through chanting and then transferring them to reading is of vital importance; it is the key to your students being able to retain the words. With use of the 3 Habits, the retention is so strong that, after being on holiday in the summer, students would return with the same bank of words. There was no fall back!

This component of the 3 Habits is done in small groups or with individual students.

- Group students according to reading level so they can all read the same book. If you have only two or three students that require this instruction, and they are all at different reading levels, you may be able to take them one at a time. You may need to have groups with a range of reading levels; in this case, each child will be given a book at his or her level, and they take turns reading one page of the book.

- Select a book at the students' instructional level.

Does tracking print with a finger impede fluency? The best way to increase fluency is to teach students the sight words through chanting and the transfer. As more and more words are read with ease, fluency improves. Finger tracking improves reading and is essential for students who do not monitor their reading.

- Have students read aloud from their books. Have them use their fingers to track the words. Pointing to each word, they practice the one-to-one match. If a student doesn't have the one-to-one match (and several won't) take her or his finger and point for the student: one point for each word, regardless of the number of syllables in the word.

- While reading, students will encounter words memorized from the high-frequency words list. While they can all chant the words in order as they appear in the list, they probably won't be able to recognize the words embedded in text.

- When the child gets to a word that he or she is able to chant from the Power Words list, but that is not recognized in the text, say, "You know this word."

- Show the child the word from the list and say, "Here it is." The student won't be able to read it.

- Immediately say, "Let's read down to it." Together, using the Power Words list in the reading duotang, start chanting down to that word. At first, you will need to start at the very top of the column (i.e., *a, and, away*), but once students get proficient at saying the words in order, you can streamline the chanting by starting at a different point. If a child is having difficulty with a word in the text that is at least midway down the column, direct the student to go up five to ten words and start chanting there instead of from the top. Chant with the child from the chosen point. Once you get the chant going, the child can join in and chant down to the desired word.

- Go back to the word in the book and say, "Let's read it again." If the student gets stuck on the word again, go to the list and repeat the procedure. Then bring the student back to the book. With students who have a hard time, you may have to repeat the procedure a couple of times.

- If the high-frequency word in the book looks different — starts with an uppercase letter, or is in a different font — follow the procedure described above. Then show the child both the word in the text and the word on the list and say, "This is the same word but… (it starts with an uppercase letter; it has a fancy *g*; etc.)" so the comparison can be seen.

Every day when you read with your struggling readers, you will help them transfer words from the list to the text.

Tips for Transferring the Words

- Be sure to transfer the words every time the opportunity arises.
- Have the students' reading duotangs handy for reference.
- Follow the script exactly. Saying "You know this word" in a positive, matter-of-fact way tells the student you believe he or she really does know it. Saying something like "Don't you remember this word?" changes the delivery to a negative phrase that is really a put down. Don't say, "Let's chant the words"; it's always "Let's read down to it."
- Use the chant every time. Don't make the chant into a song. Some teachers have tried singing the words to a particular tune, but found that students don't know where they are in the song and always have to start at the top.
- Some high-frequency words look similar, and this causes difficulty for students. For example, students who lack the visual memory often mix up *said* and *and*. When students mix up words, have a good look at them, and the similarities will become obvious. Celebrate that they are starting to pick up some visual information.
- In a guided-reading session, you may have time for just a few pages, but the precise instruction that you deliver will move these students forward.
- Be patient and praise your students and they will be successful.

Here's an example of what would take place.

How long should students track with their finger? If you have students track their reading with a finger, they will not need to be told to stop doing it. They will stop on their own when they no longer find it useful. Sometimes students will stop reading with their finger too soon, before they are able to regularly self-correct errors. Students needs to know that it is their job to make sure that what they are saying is correct. Explicit teaching is necessary. You need to make it clear that if a student points to a word and says "big," it's the student's job to check and make sure the word is "big."

You have a student who is able to chant the first column of the Power Words list. You have chanted the words on this particular day and now you are ready to do some guided reading with her. The line in the text reads *The dump truck is big.* The child points to *The* and freezes, as she cannot recognize this word. You say, "You know this word." You take the list you have handy and show her the word *the*. Then you say, "Here it is. Let's read down to it." Together you chant from the top of the column, starting with the words *a, and, away* … all the way to *the*. Stop the student there. Many kids will keep going, as they have forgotten the word you pointed to. You have the student go back to the word in the book and say, "Let's read it again." Repeat the procedure if necessary. The child will point to the word in the book and say "The." You say, "I knew you knew that word!" She loves the praise and feels great about herself. Since *The* has an uppercase *T*, you would bring the student back to the list and point to *the*; you point to *The* in the book at the same time while saying, "This is the same word. Here it has an uppercase *T* but it still says 'the'."

You tell her to keep reading. She may be able to read *dump truck* with the aid of the picture, but now she's stuck on the word *is*. Repeat the procedure. You say, "You know this word," and so on. Every time you get to a word that the child can chant from the list of high-frequency words, you help her with the transfer. This is how she takes the words she is able to chant and starts to recognize them embedded in text.

Students will begin to independently use the chant and the list words as a frame of reference. Eventually you will reach for the list as you say, "You know this word," and the child will stop you, look away, start chanting quietly, and then go back to the text and say the word. It is a really neat process to observe. I believe students come to be able to picture the words in the list, and the chant helps them to recall them. Soon they will not require the chanting, as they will know these words well, both in and out of context.

Once this process starts, where the child starts to transfer on his own, the other words will start to come quicker and more easily.

Reading Strategies

As well as finding it impossible to remember letter sounds and high-frequency words, the students who have the most trouble reading do not know what to do when they are reading and get stuck on a word. They learn to do one of two things: they freeze or they guess. Struggling students find that these strategies have worked really well for them because, in the end, we provide the word! They need to learn useful strategies (not freezing and guessing) in order to read other words they encounter.

There are lots of reading strategies; there is no shortage of strategies to choose from. I have chosen three strategies that, when taught explicitly and clearly, will solve any word almost all of the time. In fact, only the first two strategies are really used; the third is there to use "just in case."

What if a student is stuck on a word in a book — a word found in the second column of the Power Words list — and this student hasn't started chanting that list yet? Or what if a student gets to a word that is not a high-frequency word? The transfer is only for words the child is able to chant. The following strategies are used for all other words.

When the students get to words that are unfamiliar (and are not included in the words they can chant), they are coached on how to solve a word using these three strategies:

1. Say the first sound, and go back.
2. Sound it out
3. Skip it, and then go back.

Teaching the First Reading Strategy

The first strategy is a reading strategy that is usually referred to as rereading; students are usually prompted to do so with the command, "Reread." Sometimes kids don't really understand the term and often don't see the benefit. Years ago, a friend and colleague of mine suggested I prompt the kids by saying, "Say the first sound and go back." She would add, "It will come out of your mouth, like magic." When I tell the kids it works like magic, and we look at lots of examples where the right word comes flying out, their eyes go wide and they think it's pretty neat. They quickly understand that to "go back" means to read the sen-

Materials Needed:
- reading duotangs
- leveled book
- 2–10 minutes

See page 40 for Reading Strategies. Post a copy by your guided-reading table, and give the student a copy to be placed in his or her reading duotang.

From day one, all three components begin: high-frequency words, letter sounds, and reading strategies.

tence, or part of the sentence, again to gain meaning from the text. By saying the first sound of the unknown word, the choice is narrowed down.

- As you work with students in small groups or on a one-on-one basis, begin with only the first strategy. Start by telling the student that, when we are reading, it is sometimes obvious what the word will be. Give several examples of easy fill-in-the-blanks; for example, point to the child's shirt and say, "Mary is wearing a red sh_____". The child will say the word "shirt." Say enthusiastically, "How did you know? It made sense." Lots of examples will help students to understand.

- Always have the student go to meaning first when solving a word. Encourage the student to look at the pictures and think about what would make sense. Once the student understands that reading needs to make sense, prompt the first strategy: "Say the first sound and go back."

- Find places in the book you are reading where the picture supports the unknown word. Use these instances as practice with your guided-reading group; for example, a picture of a dog in a basket will yield, "The dog is in the b_____." One of your students will shout out "basket." Say, with much enthusiasm, "You're right! How did you know?" Get the kids to say with you, "Because it makes sense."

- To elaborate on the point, give examples of what wouldn't make sense. Students will find this great fun as together you think of words that don't start with *b* — "The dog is in the house," "The dog is in the principal's office" — and words that start with *b* but don't make sense — "The dog is in the bird's nest," "The dog is in the blue." Primary kids roar with laughter and begin to understand what making sense really means.

- During a guided-reading session, have a group of students practice this first strategy together. Imagine the sentence in the book reads, *Sarah lived in a red house.* One student begins to read and is stuck on the word *house.* In early lessons, the child may choose from the repertoire of bad habits (freeze or guess). Tell the student, "From now on we aren't going to freeze or guess; we are going to use our first reading strategy every time we are stuck." Prompt the student by saying, "Say the first sound and go back." If you've done lots of practice, your student will be able to follow the instruction.

- Say, "We're going to say the first sound." Then together say "h ____." Next say, "And then we go back — Sarah lived in a red h____." Go back to the student who was reading and say, "What would make sense?"; read it again. If the student makes a good attempt — for example, uses the first sound and says "home" instead of "house" — praise the student by saying, "That's a really good answer because that makes sense, but this time it's 'house'."

It is important to note here that your student is working on a lot of new things. The student is mastering sounds and high-frequency words, trying to break old habits and learn strategies. When we point out that he or she is freezing or guessing the tone needs to be supportive and light.

- Don't confuse the issue by getting into any other teaching at this point. All we want is for the student to be using the first strategy right now. If the first strategy doesn't help the student to solve the word, just tell the student the word.

- At the point where students can articulate the first strategy and are starting to execute it independently, you can prompt them when they revert to old habits by saying , "You froze when you were stuck. What can you do to help yourself?" You want them to say, "Say the first sound and go back." Say it for them if they don't, and have them repeat it. When students continually guess, point out the bad habit and say, "Everything that you say has to match the print, so what can you do instead of guessing?" Have the child say, "Say the first sound and go back."

Eventually students will use the first strategy whenever they are stuck. It is, of course, not a strategy that will work all the time, but it is important for students to use this strategy first. Students who have mastered the first strategy can move on to learning how to use the second strategy. If the first strategy doesn't help to solve the word, we teach the child the second strategy: Sound it out.

Teaching the Second Reading Strategy

As with the first strategy, it will take much modeling and prompting before a student can do this independently of you. Patience is a must, as the child has a lot to contend with.

The first two strategies are the most effective, and will enable the child to solve unknown words almost all the time. Students need to learn and perform the strategies in order: the first strategy is all about meaning, and is the quickest way to solve a word, so fluency will not be hampered; meaning will not always help to solve a word, so the second strategy offers the next best way to solve a word.

Some children are very good at sounding out words and are in the habit of using only this strategy. It is important to tell the child that sounding out is a great strategy, but that it is not the first thing we will do when we're stuck. The child needs to know to always try the first strategy before trying the second. The child should be able to articulate the two strategies that can be used when a reader is stuck on a word.

- Imagine the line in the book reads *The cat looked at the black fish*. The child is stuck on *black*. The child can chant the first column of the Power Words list, but *black* is found in the second column, so you will not do the transfer. The child tries the first strategy, but still does not know the word. When the first strategy doesn't help the student, say, "We always say the first sound and go back. But if that doesn't help, then we use our second strategy — sound it out."

- Repeat the prompt: "Sound it out." Instruct the student to run a finger under the sounds as he or she reads, "b-l-a-ck." Praise the student and ask the group, "What did _____ do when he was stuck?" Together say, "He said the first sound and went back. And then he sounded it out."

- Instruct the student to continue reading.

Perhaps there's a child in the group who struggles to sound out words. This is not uncommon and will require explicit instruction from you. If the rest of the group doesn't need this help, work with the child separately on this.

- Start with one-syllable words the student knows that can be phonetically decoded, such as *cat, dog*. Write these simple words one at a time and have the child point to each sound as he or she moves across the word.

- Move into more difficult words when the student is ready — words like *must, blast*. Keep working with the child to master this skill and it will eventually come. I have had students who had a very difficult time with this, but we kept working and eventually they were able to sound words out.

- If the student uses both strategies with ease and still cannot read the word, praise the student's efforts and tell the student the word.

Letter Combinations and the Second Reading Strategy

As students master the letter sounds and move on to the letter combinations, the prompt for this second strategy will change. As they work on the digraphs and blends and try to decode words, encourage them to "Look for what needs to stay together and sound it out." This change in wording is necessary when we want them to attend to the combinations.

At this stage, students are ready to learn more about the print they see. If your student is trying to solve a word, has tried the first strategy and is now using the second strategy — Sound it out — you can let the student try, then point out the silent *e* at the end of word. Say, "This *e* is silent and makes no noise at the end of a word. Its job is to tell the vowel to say its name." As an example, you would point to the *a* in the word and say, "This letter's name is 'a' so here it says 'ay'. Let's point to the sounds, and now sound it out."

The letter-combinations stage is also when you can also discuss word endings. If a child is reading endings with no errors, there is no need for discussion. If a child says "play" instead of "playing" when reading, and does not correct the error, cover the *ing* and say, "This says play." Remove your finger and say, "When we add *ing* it says 'playing'. Let's read it again." After much modeling (and when the first reading strategy doesn't help), tell the child to cover the endings with a finger and then apply the second strategy. As with silent *e*, prefixes, and suffixes, teach word endings only within the context of the text as you come across it. Do not spend a lot of time teaching it; just be matter-of-fact about it. Students will learn more about this as they read and encounter it.

Teaching the Third Reading Strategy

When students can use the first two strategies independently, move on to the third: Skip it, and then go back

- Tell students, "Sometimes we can read the rest of the sentence, and this will help us figure out the unknown word." Explain that this is not a strategy we use very often, as the first two strategies will solve most words.

- Imagine the sentence is *John lost his mom's gold ring.* The student reads up to the word *gold* and stops. The student executes the first two strategies to no avail. Prompt the student to use the third strategy by saying, "Skip it and go back."

- Work with the child by pointing to the word *gold* and saying, "The first two strategies did not help. Let's skip this word and read on, and see if we can figure out what that word is."

- Have the student read to the end of the sentence. Then say, "Let's go back to the beginning of the sentence and read it again."

- Have the student read the sentence. If she or he is still stuck, ask, "I wonder what the word is. John lost his mom's g_____ ring. What kind of ring could it be? We know it starts with the *g* sound."

- Lots of practice and modeling is required. Remind your student that this is a third strategy, another tool to use if the first two don't work.

You need to be clear with your students about your expectations. They need to know that it is their responsibility as readers to help themselves at difficulty

Although you might use other strategies — e.g., prompting long and short vowel sounds; pointing out smaller words within the word — struggling students seem to fare better when they have exact rules to follow in order when they are stuck. As they get used to using the strategies independently, and get familiar with tricks in the English language, they will put it all together, reading with fluency and ease.

Self-monitoring occurs when the reader is checking her- or himself for accuracy. The reader often notices when mistakes are made and attempts to fix them. He or she double checks words from time to time to be sure they are correct. Readers who self-monitor do not look at the teacher to see if they are correct; they check the text to be sure.

(use strategies), and match everything they say to the print (track print carefully and fix errors). Eventually students will be able to recognize the high-frequency words while reading. They will become proficient at using the reading strategies to tackle unfamiliar words.

Tips for Teaching Reading Strategies

- It is important for students to point to each word as they read. You don't want to do the pointing for them — they need to learn independence. Some worry that the fluency will be affected if a child is encouraged to point when reading. What is more important to consider is what will affect the child's success in reading. If a student continues to guess or to not track print properly, that student will not be a successful reader. Keep the child pointing if she or he is not self-monitoring and you will find that, in the end, the child will be able to read accurately and fluently.
- Lots of practice will need to take place for students to start using the first strategy correctly. They will need lots of praise and encouragement.
- For some students, freezing and guessing is quite a strong habit that takes time to break. Keep telling them, "Say the first sound and go back." You need to point out when they freeze or guess; tell them to throw these strategies in the garbage and to put their new first strategy in their pocket ready to pull out when needed.
- These strategies need to be mastered one at a time. The teacher and student need to practice together several times before the student can be asked to apply them independently. They need to be rehearsed repeatedly.
- Never suggest the use of strategies for high-frequency words that the student can chant. Do the transfer.
- There are times when a reader will use all strategies and still not be able to figure out the word. Such is the nature of English. For example, a student may get stuck on the word *know*. Allow the student the chance to try to figure it out by using the three strategies. Once they have tried, you can tell them the word. Say, "Some words are funny. In this word, the *k* is silent."
- Students may find some words harder than others to remember. For example, students often say "he" instead of "here" even though it is on the Power Words list. Always bring them back to the list to do the transfer, but you may want to point out the two words so the student can compare and see the difference. Students also seem to struggle with *they*, in the Level 2 column of the word list. If students have mastered this column but still struggle to read *they* in text, bring them back to the list and start the chant just prior to the word.
- Increase your students' metacognition by asking key questions (*How did you know the word was* house? *What can you do to help yourself?*), and by making explicit statements about what went well (*You said the first sound and went back!*) and what didn't go so well (freezing or guessing).

Remember: the most important thing you are teaching your students is to help themselves when they get to something they don't know. You want your students to be able to read whether or not you are sitting beside them.

Reading Strategies

1. Say the 1st sound and go back.

2. Sound it out.

3. Skip the word and then go back.

Note: once the combinations chant begins, change Reading Strategy 2 to "Look for what needs to stay together and sound it out."

Habit 3: Assessment

3

How do you find time to instruct and assess your struggling students every day? You begin with your daily guided-reading session, as described as part of Habit 2. During the guided-reading session and any time you listen to your students read, you are observing — assessing on the run. Find spare minutes to listen again during the day to the students who are furthest behind, outside of the guided reading session. Just listen to a couple of pages and observe what each student is doing, offer guidance as needed, and let your students know what they are doing. Are they freezing or guessing? Are they starting with the first strategy to help themselves at difficulty? Are they looking at the pictures and thinking about the meaning? This only takes a couple of minutes, but will give you a chance to observe and move each student along by giving them all very specific information and reminders.

I have been observing the reading process for years. When we commit to student success, I believe that all kids can learn to read. For some students, it might be a longer journey, but all students get there. What makes your teaching more effective? Part of what makes you more effective when teaching reading, or anything else, is regular assessment and analysis. The more we reflect on our teaching, the more effective we become.

Teachers who regularly assess their students and analyze the results are able to get students reading at grade level faster. The value of the assessment (and analysis) cannot be overstated. Without it, the child may make progress, but time will be wasted in keeping the student at the same book level and teaching the student what he or she already knows. It is also important to track students to be sure they are reading books at their instructional level.

The Reading Check

The Reading Check is easily scheduled into your timetable. It needs to be administered at least weekly for your students reading below grade level. One day a week, take some time during guided reading and complete the Reading Check instead. Some teachers find time at other points during the day. By looking carefully at your timetable, you'll find the time you need.

What do we need to do to ensure that we are succeeding at teaching students to read? We observe, assess (through observation), and instruct students during daily guided-reading sessions. We also need to listen to our students read, formally record what they do, and analyze our recordings on a weekly basis. The Reading Check (adapted from the Running Record) is your "assessment for learning" tool that informs you as to what your student is doing and not doing, and clearly indicates what the next step is.

Formative assessments such as the Reading Check are vital to student success. In order for classroom teachers to be able to complete assessments on a regular basis, assessments need to be quick and easy to do. The Reading Check is a quick but valuable tool that gives you the vital information you need. The student reads for a few minutes. If you have more time, listen to more text; however, just a few minutes will allow you to see how the student is progressing.

How often should students be formally assessed? Every day would be ideal, but this is not always possible. Therefore, the answer is that you should assess your most struggling students as often as you can, and at least once a week.

The Reading Check
- is recorded in the same way as a Running Record, but students are not penalized for repeated errors or proper nouns
- permits the teacher to set the stage for success, provide specific prompts as needed, and offer encouragement
- ensures the student is working at his or her instructional level.

When the Reading Check is analyzed, it enables you to see exactly what reading component needs extra attention: are students transferring the sight words to text, remembering the letter sounds, and using reading strategies when they are stuck? The Reading Check and Analysis highlights what the child is doing well, and where the area for growth lies for the teacher and/or the student.

The Reading Check analysis
- allows you to see exactly what the student is doing and not doing
- is very precise, as it zones in on the three reading components — high-frequency words, letter sounds, reading strategies — and determines where the weakness lies
- guides your instruction, as it magnifies the problem area and allows you to reflect on your instruction to correctly deliver the next step required

In order to read, a child needs to know letter sounds, high-frequency words, and how to use strategies for unknown words. You need to know what your student is doing and not doing so you can fine-tune your instruction. If you regularly assess your students, they will move forward quickly, as you check to see what the next step is.

- Work one-on-one with a student to do a Reading Check. Have a book ready that you believe is at the student's instructional level.

Materials Needed:
- a leveled book
- Reading Check Recording Sheet (page 50)
- Reading Check: Errors and Analysis sheet (page 51)

When doing Reading Checks, students know that your expectations are high. They know that you believe in them. Through your words, body language, and enthusiasm you have conveyed that you are proud of them and know they are smart. They know what their job as readers entails. They have been set up for success.

- Begin by telling the student how impressed you are with his or her progress. Tell the student that you would like to hear him or her read a couple of pages; assure the student that you know he or she will do a great job.

- Ask, "Are you going to guess or freeze if you are stuck on a word?" Go over the strategies the student has learned thusfar. Remind the student about the responsibilities of a reader by saying, "Remember, it's your job to help yourself when you're stuck. It's also your job to be sure that whatever you say matches the print."

- Using the Reading Check Recording Sheet (page 50) begin as you would when completing a Running Record. Write the student's name, name of book, and level.
  - Use check marks to represent the words the student is reading correctly.
  - When the student makes an error, write what the child says on top and what the text says on the bottom.
  - When the student inserts or omits words, record them and mark them as errors.
  - If the student freezes ask, "How can you help yourself?" If there is no response, wait a few seconds and then give the student the word. Just as with a Running Record, mark a *T* if the student needs to be told the word.
  - If the student guesses at a word and pauses, wait a second and then prompt by saying, "Whatever you say has to match."
  - Indicate if the child says any sounds in a word or repeats words or lines.

- After the student has read a couple of lines, stop to encourage and praise the student by saying, "You're doing a great job because you are using your strategies" or "because you know it's your job to look carefully."

- As the student continues to read and use the strategies when stuck, smile to help the student relax, and offer encouragement such as saying, "Great job."

Use the wording of the prompts provided here. The prompts help you create an environment that is stress-free and allows the child to perform at her or his best. Using these specific prompts offers more insight about your student. For example, if a student freezes and says nothing, we would normally tell the child the word, knowing nothing but that the student did not help herself or himself when stuck. If we prompt, we see exactly why the student froze. Is the student able to execute the strategies? Is the student unsure of the letter sounds? Is the student trying to retrieve the high-frequency word? We then know exactly how to help the student.

The Reading Check can be as quick as a couple of minutes, or longer if time permits. From the short interaction, you will glean much information:

- if the student is able to transfer the high-frequency words to text
- if the student knows the sounds of the letters
- if the student can execute the reading strategies successfully
- if the student is reverting to guessing at words or freezing

The quick assessment will let you know the next steps for the student, what to focus on in continued teaching.

On the Reading Check: Errors and Analysis sheet (page 51) errors are recorded and analyzed to see what component is most likely required for the child to solve a word. For each error we ask if the student needs

- more help with the high-frequency words?
- more help with letter sounds (individual letters or combinations)?
- more help using strategies?

If more work is needed with the high-frequency words (this would involve the chanting and transfer) mark the *Analysis* as being *HF*. If more work is needed because the student did not know an individual sound or combination, mark *L* in the *Analysis* column. If more work is needed with the strategies, mark *S*.

Once you complete the analysis, you need to deliver the information to the child. How effectively you are able to do this will have a big impact on the student's progress. Keep the message brief but precise. The student needs to understand exactly what he or she needs to do in order to improve. It is best to give the student the feedback soon after he or she has read. You may be able to analyze the errors and conference with the child later the same day. When you first start the Reading Checks it will take time to get used to the analysis. As you gain experience, you will be able to analyze the errors very quickly (even as the child is reading) and provide timely feedback. Be sure to begin with what went well with the three reading components (i.e., having a bank of high-frequency words, remembering to look for letter combinations, execution of reading strategies in order) and give examples from your record. In a supportive way, explain exactly what the student needs to do to improve. Have the student then explain to you the exact small step he or she needs to work on.

Recording and Analyzing Reading Checks

Sample A: Reading Check Recording and Analysis

page	
2	✓ ✓ ✓ ✓ ✓ <u>mother</u> mom ✓ ✓ ✓ ✓ ✓ ✓ ✓ ✓ <u>house</u> home
3	✓ ✓ ✓ ✓ ✓ ✓ <u>far</u> fast

Error #	Record of Errors	Analysis: HF/L/S
1	<u>mother</u> mom	S
2	<u>house</u> home	S
3	<u>far</u> fast	S

Following the Reading Check A above, we see that the child made his first error with the word *mom*. Under *Record of Errors* we wrote the following:

<u>mother</u>
mom

What component did this child most likely need in order to read the word correctly? Looking at the error, we ask ourselves if *mom* is a high-frequency word from the list that the student can chant? The answer is no, so more work on the high-frequency words wouldn't have helped. Did he not read the word correctly because he didn't know the sounds? This is not evident. Did he not read the word correctly because he didn't use strategies? Yes; we know from the recording sheet that he did not say the first word and go back, nor did he attempt any other strategies. Under the heading *Analysis*, you would write a *S*. If the student had used the strategies, he probably would have been able to solve the word.

The second error is written on the analysis sheet as

<u>house</u>
home

We look again at the high-frequency words, letter sounds, and strategies. Which component would have most likely helped him read the word correctly? The word *home* is not a high-frequency word, and there is no evidence that he didn't remember the sounds, as we did not observe him breaking down the word — so that's not it. He did not use strategies to help himself; he just guessed so the letter *S* is marked under the *Analysis* heading. Even though the teacher prompted the student with "What you say has to match," he did nothing and continued to read.

The third error is marked as this:

far
‾‾‾
fast

The three reading components — high-frequency words, letter sounds, and reading strategies — are all a child needs to be able to decode.

The third error also occurred because the student did not use strategies. Perhaps he has been taught only the first strategy at this point. But we would expect to see him use it if it was mastered.

How does this analysis help to guide our instruction? We look for what most likely occurred, according to what the student did while reading. The student clearly is reading the high-frequency words he encounters, so this component is fine. He did not indicate that he had trouble sounding out any words. But three times an error occurred because he did not use strategies.

The teacher now knows how to move this student forward. The next time they read together, the teacher needs to discuss her findings with the child and say, "Every time you read, it's your job to use your strategies each time you're unsure of the word. Guessing won't help you, strategies will." During the next guided reading session, all three components (sight words, letters, and strategies) will be taught, but the teacher will pay particular attention to how she is teaching the strategies and what the student is doing when he is stuck. If he doesn't use the strategies, the teacher must stop him and instruct him to do so in a supportive way. The teacher needs to determine if this student is forgetting the strategies or is stuck on his old habits. Since the teacher prompted him, and he did nothing, it is likely that he is not recalling what the strategies are. This student needs to go back to the first strategy and master it before moving on to the second strategy.

Sample B: Reading Check Recording and Analysis

Sample B: Reading Check Recording and Analysis

page	
2	✓ ✓ ✓ ✓ ✓ ___–___ ✓ ✓ ✓ like
3	✓ ✓ ✓ ✓ ✓ ✓ ◄——————— r ✓ ✓ ✓ s/s-h-o-u-t shouted ✓ ✓ ✓ ✓ ✓ ✓ ✓ ___–___ ✓ ✓ ✓ ate T

Error #	Record of Errors	Analysis: HF/L/S
1	$\dfrac{-}{\text{like}}$	HF
2	$\dfrac{\text{s/s-h-o-u-t}}{\text{shouted}}$	L
3	$\dfrac{-}{\text{ate}\quad\text{T}}$	HF

Sample B is another example of how to analyze errors. The first error is marked like this:

$$\frac{-}{\text{like}}$$

The student froze and said nothing. This is a high-frequency word that she chants, so it is clear she is not transferring it to text. The teacher would mark a *HF* under the *Analysis* heading. If it had been a high-frequency word that this student hadn't got to chanting yet, it should have been treated as an unknown word and an opportunity to use the reading strategies.

The second error is

$$\frac{\text{s/s-h-o-u-t}}{\text{shouted}}$$

The student said the "s" sound. Then she started again and said all the sounds separately. Which component did she need the most? She did not recognize *sh* and *ou*. The teacher would mark *L* under the *Analysis* heading. If the student did not know the sounds, as is the case here, the component is *L*; if she had indicated that she had problems sounding out words, the focus would have been strategies.

The third error is

$$\frac{-}{\text{ate}\quad\text{T}}$$

The teacher would mark a *HF*, as *ate* is part of the list that the student chants. She can chant the word but did not transfer it to text. If the student had not reached that column yet in her chanting, we would expect her to tackle this word as an unknown. If she had paused, it would be likely that she was trying to retrieve the word from the list but was unsuccessful. The teacher waited a second or two, and then told the student the word and marked it as a told (*T*), which is recorded as an error.

When we analyze the student's errors we discover that we need to work harder at teaching her the high-frequency words. We need her chanting the list words more often, and we need to be sure we are doing the transfer for this student at every opportunity; i.e., every time we come across a high-frequency word while reading (a word that she is able to chant), we bring her back to the list to chant down to it, and then back to the book. The words *ate* and *like* are both on the Level 2 list. Perhaps this student is able to chant the Level 1 and Level 2 columns, and is working on the Level 3 column. We keep going with Level 3 and add one word a day, but we also must take time with her each day and have her point to each word starting with Level 1 until she is able to transfer the words from Level 1 to text. We tell her to look carefully as she "reads" the words so she can remember what they look like. Then we spend extra time at Level 2.

We also see that this student is not recognizing the letter combinations when reading text. We know that she knows her individual letters and has just started with the combinations. We need to keep chanting the combinations and make sure she attends to all combinations when she reads her books. If she doesn't recognize them as she reads, we bring her back to the combinations sheet and have her chant to the combination, then go back to the text and ask her what the two letters say when we keep them together.

The analysis allows you to see what the child is doing, and to reflect on your instruction. Are you delivering the components as described in chapter 2? If a component needs work, it might be a reflection on how you are delivering it. Are you approaching the child in a way that conveys your belief in him or her?

Most errors will indicate which of the three reading components would have helped the child read the word correctly. This, in turn, guides us clearly as to how to help the child move forward in her reading progress.

There are words that this student will eventually be able to read when she's exposed to them as she reads more and more texts. Words like *gnaw* and *hyena* are probably not going to be solved by the components, but that's okay. Words like this are recorded as errors, but nothing is marked under the *Analysis* heading (unless the student didn't attempt the word by using strategies). Even though the child will probably not be able to read the word, we still expect the child to tackle them as unknown words and use strategies.

The main focus during your guided reading is always to teach the letter sounds, sight words, and reading strategies. The Reading Check and Analysis will show you how well you are instructing in these three areas. If your student is not clear about letter sounds, is not transferring high-frequency words, or is not using the reading strategies, teach all three components, but spend extra time on the particular area of need.

Scoring the Reading Check

The Reading Check needs to be scored. Words that are corrected by the student are not counted as errors. In a Reading Check, students are not penalized for repeated errors or proper nouns.

The purpose of scoring a Reading Check is to determine the student's instructional level. If a student is penalized for repeated errors, the score could be lowered significantly just because of one word. The score would not represent the child's instructional level.

To get a Reading Check score, the correct words are divided by the total number of words and multiplied by 100.

$$\text{Reading Check Score} = \frac{\text{Correct Words}}{\text{Total Words}} \times 100$$

For example, a child made 5 errors and read 75 words in total.

$$\frac{\text{Correct Words } 70}{\text{Total Words } 75} \times 100 = 93$$

The student read 93% of the words correctly. Since this student scored 93%, he was reading the book at the instructional level — the book is not too hard and not too easy.

A score between 90% and 94% is instructional level. It is at this instructional level that a student should be reading. An instructional-level text will keep the child motivated and feeling successful. He is not frustrated, as there are not too many words he doesn't know. But he has a few words to work on. He is required to practice using the strategies you are teaching him to master.

If a child scores less than 90%, the text is too hard for that student. Work on the problem areas. Read over the components the student needs to focus on to be sure you are teaching them correctly.

The score will guide you as to the level at which you should have your student reading. Regardless of the score, use the information you gain to guide your next move and determine what you need to concentrate on.

Is it necessary to ask students questions about what they've read to check comprehension? When students read, you can tell if they comprehend by looking at the errors and self-corrections being made. If a student stops and self-corrects so that the reading makes sense, that student is demonstrating comprehension. But if a student makes mistakes and is clearly not using meaning, I have found that a simple chat is required. Students sometimes get preoccupied by concentrating on what they sound like when reading for the teacher. They get nervous and don't concentrate on the text. The student needs to realize that it is his or her job as a reader to be sure that what he or she says makes sense. An example or two may be necessary, and then there should be no more confusion.

Many schools use data walls to track reading levels. A teacher named Sue Keating introduced me to the personal and portable Reading Level Tracking Sheet (page 52) that makes it easy to track your students' reading levels. Simply write the names of all the students in your class (not just your strugglers) along the side and write the book levels along the top. You can color in the squares as your students move up levels, to see at a glance how each child is progressing. Every week or so you might use a different color so you can see growth in a given period of time. The advantage to having all the information on one sheet is that it's easy to quickly see how your students are doing: who needs more help, who hasn't moved in a while, who hasn't been assessed lately. The fact that the Tracking Sheet is portable allows you to take it with you to do a quick assessment. It allows you to have it handy as you reevaluate your groupings and discuss your students with the resource teacher and colleagues.

The Reading Check is a great tool. While the teacher is able to extract valuable information, the student does not even realize he or she is being assessed, as the teacher converses with the student during the assessment. Research indicates that the anxiety many students experience from test-like situations affects the nervous system and the brain's ability to retain, recall, and learn new information. If we are able to reduce stress and replace the feelings of anxiety with feelings of confidence, support, and contentment, students are able to think more clearly and their brains function at an optimal level.

Some teachers have asked about how to improve errors associated with poor grammar. If a child is exposed to poor grammar at home, good modeling at school will correct this.

Sample Reading Level Tracking Sheet

Name/Level	1	2	3	4	5	6	7	8	9	10
Student A	▓	▓	▓	▓						
B	▓	▓	▓	▓	▓	▓	▓			
C	▓	▓								
D	▓									
E	▓	▓	▓	▓	▓	▓	▓	▓	▓	▓

Tips for Using the Reading Check

- After each Reading Check, praise the child for what went well. Provide feedback about the area that needs attention as soon as possible.
- When scoring a Reading Check, remember that students are not penalized for repeated errors or proper nouns.
- Record the score at the bottom of the Reading Check Sheet.
- A Reading Check score between 90% and 94% is instructional level. It is at this instructional level that a student should be reading.

Reading Check Recording Sheet

page	

Reading Check: Errors and Analysis

Error #	Record of Errors	Analysis: HF/L/S

Total Errors: _____ Word Count: _____ Score: _____ (Easy/Instructional/Hard)

Notes: _____

_____

Next Step: HF – Needs more work on transferring high-frequency words
L – Needs more work on individual letter sounds or combinations
S – Needs more work on using the strategies

Reading Level Tracking Sheet

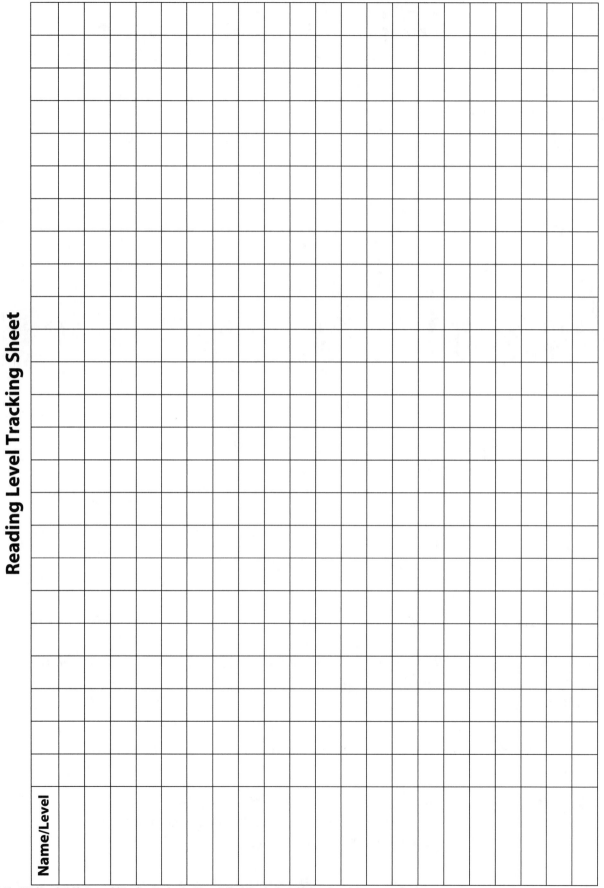

Name/Level

Diagnostic Assessment : Starting the 3 Habits

Before you begin to implement the 3 Habits, you need to begin with diagnostic assessments to determine a starting point for instruction.

It is necessary to assess your students to see which ones will require extra assistance; using the 3 Habits, you can differentiate your instruction to suit the needs of all your students.

- Find out what your students know and don't know. Teachers teaching beyond Junior Kindergarten have the luxury of talking to previous teachers and using the previous year's data to begin to gauge their students' level.

- Put your students into one of three categories using your class list: Above Grade Level, At Grade Level, or Below Grade Level. All students will need to be assessed, but begin with students believed to be working below grade level. Your list can be fine-tuned and changed as you get to know your students better.

- Use a Diagnostic Assessment Recording Sheet (page 57) for each student. Fill in the student information.

Part 1: Observation Record

You want to know at which level your students are reading, so you must complete a diagnostic assessment of reading. The Observation Record (adapted from the Running Record) is similar to a Reading Check, but no prompts are permitted. It is used to determine the instructional level of reading for your students. The Observation Record records repeated errors with the same word as one error, and does not penalize for mistakes with proper nouns. For example, if the child encounters the word *out* three times in the Observation Record and is unable to read it correctly each time, it is counted as one error instead of three errors. If the child cannot pronounce a proper noun correctly, the name is just given to the child, and no error is recorded.

- To complete an Observation Record you begin in the same way as you would a Running Record. Have your student read a book you believe will be at the correct instructional level. Some leveled readers are quite lengthy. You don't have to have the child read the whole book — 80 to 100 words will suffice.

- Use check marks to represent the words read. Read the title for the child. Have the child begin to read; use checkmarks on the Observation Record to represent words read correctly. The placement of your checkmarks will mimic the words in the book. If the first page has three words, record the page number and place three checkmarks beside it if the student reads them all correctly. The next page's checks would appear underneath that line, and so on down the page.

- When your student makes an error, draw a horizontal line in place of the check mark; write what the student says on top of the line and what the text reads on the below.

- When the student inserts or omits words, these are recorded as errors. For insertions, record what the child said on top on the line and record a dash below the line. When the student omits a word, the dash is above and the word from the text is below the line.

- If the student freezes, wait a few seconds and give the student the word; this is recorded as an error. Mark *T* below the line.

- If the child rereads at any point, indicate where the repeat took place with an *r* and draw a line with an arrow indicating how far back the child went.

- If the child goes back and corrects any errors, they are marked as self-corrections and no errors are recorded.

Observation Record Sample

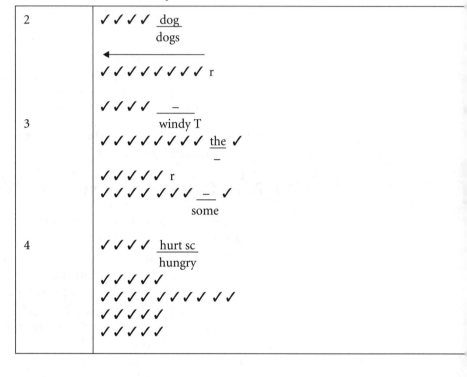

Total Errors: _____ Word Count: _____ Score: _____ (Easy/Instructional/Hard)

See the example of an Observation Record above. The child began reading, read four words correctly, and then said "dog" instead of *dogs* (first error). The student's answer is recorded above the line; the text from the book is below. The child read the next line correctly, and then went back and read it again. This shows us that the child is probably monitoring her reading and making sure that what she said is correct. On the next line the student got stuck on the word *windy*. After a couple of seconds, the teacher told the child the word. This is recorded as an error, and a *T* is marked at the bottom because the teacher told the student the word. The child continued to read, and inserted the word *the*. A dash is marked below to indicate that the child added this word while reading and it is recorded as an error. On the next line, the child reread one word, so an *r* is marked beside that word. The next error was when the child omitted the word *some*. Then she substituted *hurt* for *hungry*, which would have been an error, but she corrected it. A *sc* is marked to indicate that the child self-corrected, and it is not counted as an error.

Complete an Observation Record for all your students, beginning with those who are working below grade level. Use the Observation Record Sheet on page

58, and circle the word *Diagnostic*. Follow the Guide to Recording and Scoring on page 61.

Score the Observation Record as you would a Reading Check (see page 47). The correct words are divided by the total number of words and multiplied by 100. Record the score at the bottom of the Observation Record sheet. Select texts for the student to read from the book level where the student scores between 90% and 94%. This is the level that is just right for the child — not too challenging, and not too easy. The child will be able to read much of the text, but will come across some unknown words; these will enable the student to practice reading strategies. If a student scores less than 90% on the Observation Record, have this student read an easier book until you find the instructional level. A book that is too easy scores 95% or higher.

The Observation Record will determine who is in need of the program; i.e., all students who are not scoring at instructional level on grade-leveled books. You will move on to take the assessment of the high-frequency words and letter sounds (Parts 2 and 3 of the Diagnostic Assessment) for students reading below grade level.

Part 2: High-Frequency Words

- Using the Power Words list (pages 20–21), have the student begin with the Level 1 words and read as many words as he or she can. If the child can read all the words in a column, mark a check under that column heading on the Diagnostic Assessment Recording Sheet. If the child can't read any words, leave it blank. Have the student read down the column of words; write the last word he or she knows under the correct column. For example: John knows all the words in the Level 1 column and can read as far down as the word *brown* in the Level 2 column; you will put a check under *Level 1* and write *brown* under *Level 2* on the Recording Sheet. It is recorded as follows:

Level 1	Level 2	Level 3	Level 4	Level 5
✓	brown			

- If the student recognizes a word further down the column, don't record it. You are checking to see if the student can read the words in order so you have a starting point to begin teaching.

- If the student was not able to read the words fluently, do not check the column as being successfully read. If the student was sounding out the words, do not check the column as successfully read.

Here's another example: This student was able to read many words in order in the Level 1 list. When she got to the word *jump*, she did not recognize it immediately and had to sound it out. The word before *jump* is *it*, and that is what is recorded as the last word she was able to read, as follows:

Level 1	Level 2	Level 3	Level 4	Level 5
it				

Part 3: Letter Sounds

- Have your student recite the individual letter sounds using the Student Letter Sounds sheet (page 59). On your Diagnostic Assessment Recording Sheet, mark unknown letter sounds with a dot (not an x), and mark nothing for known sounds.

- Don't concern yourself with the letter names. You are looking for the building blocks for reading — the letter sounds.

- Check to see if students know their short vowel sounds, hard *g* and hard *c* sounds — the long vowel sounds, soft *g* and *c* will come later. If the student says the long "o" sound, ask if he or she knows the other sound the *o* makes. If the student doesn't know, in the space write an *o* with a macron above it to indicate long sound. Mark a dot to indicate that this child needs to learn the short vowel sounds. If the student gives the soft sounds for *g* and/or *c*, ask if he or she knows the other sound these letters make. Make a note of this.

- If your student knows all of the letter sounds, have the student recite the combinations on the Student Combinations sheet (page 60). This is, of course, not an exhaustive list of combinations, but knowing these particular letter combinations brings students into late primary reading. Record the information on the Diagnostic Assessment Recording Sheet in the same way as the individual letter sounds. If the student doesn't know the letter sounds, there is no need to test the combinations at this point. You already know your starting point for instruction.

With the diagnostic done, you know who your struggling readers are and what their strengths and areas for growth are.

Summative Assessment : Discharging Students

When struggling students reach an instructional reading level that is at grade level, it is time to discharge them. The only summative assessment that is required is an assessment of their reading. Once they are at this level, you will find that they do not require prompting during the regular Reading Checks you've been doing; they understand their responsibilities at a reader.

For this summative assessment, use an Observation Record and follow the same procedure as the diagnostic assessment. Use the Observation Record Sheet (page 58) and circle the word *Summative*. As you do the Observation Record, do not provide prompts, but feel free to interject with praise — just keep it brief so as not to distract the reader. Since your student is used to being assessed by you, and is used to your prompts, spend time beforehand explaining how this assessment will be different and do practice runs. The student needs to know that you are doing the assessment in this way because you believe he or she is independent and doesn't require prompting. You set the stage for success before this assessment by reminding the student of how smart and what a great reader he or she is. You review the expectations together.

Use the Student Discharge Sheet (page 62) to fill out the discharge information.

If a student scores hard (less than 90%) on the Observation Record, have a look at the text in the book. Has the student read that type of genre before? Should another book at that level be tried? You may want to assess your student again the next day using a different book.

Diagnostic Assessment Recording Sheet

Date _____   Name of Student _____

Teacher _____

Part 1: Observation Record

Reading Level _____ Score _____

Part 2: High-Frequency Words

Level 1	Level 2	Level 3	Level 4	Level 5

Part 3: Individual Letter Sounds

R	G	M	S	Y	B	H	N	T	Z	I	L	D	J	U	X	O	V	Q	A	C	F	E	K	P	W

r	g	m	s	y	b	h	n	t	z	i	l	d	j	u	x	o	v	q	a	c	f	e	k	p	w

Combinations

sh	th	ch	er	ir	ar	ou	ow	ow	ea	ee	ay	ew	oy	oi	oo	ur	oa

Observation Record: Diagnostic or Summative

page	

Total Errors: _____ Word Count: _____ Score: _____ (Easy/Instructional/Hard)

Student Letter Sounds

R G M S Y B H N T

Z I L D J U X O V

Q A C F E K P W

r g m s y b h n t

z i l d j u x o v

q a c f e k p w

Student Combinations

sh	th	ch
er	ir	ar
ou	ow	ow
ea	ee	ay
ew	oy	oi
oo	ur	oa

Guide to Recording and Scoring

Reading Check

Errors
- Substitutions for words: write what the student says on top and the word in the text on the bottom.
- Word omissions or insertions of extra words:
  - Put a dash in for the omission on the top and the word from the text at the bottom.
  - For insertions, put the word from the text at the top and a dash at the bottom.
- Words given by the teacher (Tolds): Put a dash on top and write a T at the bottom

Allowable Prompts from the Teacher:
- Used when child freezes: "How can you help yourself?"
- Used after child guesses: "Remember — what you say has to match the text."
- The teacher is encouraged to praise the student through body language and short phrases such as, "Good job."

Self-Corrections and Same-Word Errors:
- When a student self-corrects, the original error is not counted as an error: write *sc* beside the original error.
- If a student has made an error with a word and then encounters the word again and makes an error, you count only one error in total at the end of the Reading Check.

Word Count
- The title is given to the student by the teacher and is not counted as part of the total word count.

Observation Record: Diagnostic and Summative Assessments

Same as above except
- Prompts are not allowed

Scoring

90–94%: Instructional
Less than 90%: Hard
Greater that 94%: Easy

Student Discharge Sheet

Date _____

Teacher _____   School _____

....

Name of Student _____

Date of Entry _____

Entry Reading Level _____   Score _____

Date of Discharge _____

Discharge Reading Level _____   Score _____

4

Implementing the Habits

Before you begin to use the 3 Habits, be sure that you are ready to empower your students to reach their full potential. In other words, it is vital that everything you do and say indicates that you truly believe in your students.

The 3 Habits have been effectively used with students from Junior Kindergarten to Grade 8. For the early grades (JK to Grade 1), it is used as part of the learn-to-read program. From Grades 2 to 8 it is used as an intervention by classroom and resource teachers to advance the reading process for students who lag behind.

Fine-Tuning

As you get familiar with all components of the 3 Habits and work with your struggling students every day, you will better understand how they think and how you can help them. You will be an expert on their reading progress and will know how and when to move each child forward. Most students will accelerate quickly, but some will take more time. Don't let anything shake you from your belief that all your students will be successful.

Once you've implemented all the reading components into your daily routine, you are ready to do some reflection and look a little more closely at your students, yourself, and your scheduling.

Are you monitoring your students' progress regularly? Are the Reading Check and Analysis being done at least once a week?

Are you analyzing the Reading Check carefully so that you can find the next step for your students to practice during your guided-reading groups? After several Reading Checks of a particular student, information will emerge. A student might know all letter sounds, be transferring the words, and be using strategies consistently; however, perhaps the student is not applying the rule for silent *e*. Generally you teach the rules with silent *e*, soft *g* and *c*, etc., as you come across them in text. If your student is doing well with all components but this is hampering success, a mini-lesson may be required. Talk to the student about what you've discovered from the Reading Check and Analysis. Tell the student what he or she is doing and what he or she needs to do in order to read independently as you come across these things in the text of books. And, just as importantly, tell the student about all the great things he or she is doing and how proud you are of him or her.

Are you regularly balancing your schedule, finding spare minutes, rearranging your reading groups as needed? A student in one group may be advancing quickly and need to join another group for guided reading. As groups change, the number of groups may change too. You need to check the time you have for guided reading and see how you can best meet the needs of all of your students.

If one student needs more practice chanting the words, you have to organize your schedule to find some extra time, look at bringing in volunteers, or make more use of parent involvement (See page 67 for more on involving parents.). Your guided-reading groups and your schedule will change many times as your students' needs change.

Are you conveying your belief in each child by words and body language? Is there is a student that is not making the gains you had hoped for? Have a look at the diagnostic assessments you completed before implementing the 3 Habits. Look at the Reading Check this student last completed. Celebrate the growth. If the student has memorized words in order, this is progress. If the student is transferring a word or two to text, this is progress. Have a look at chapter 1 again and be sure you are setting the child up for success.

Are your students progressing, but in need of some detailed application of the 3 Habits? Here are some specific ways I have found to fine-tune your instruction:

- When a student is proficient at using all strategies, that student may benefit from an extra tip when reading multisyllabic words. After trying the first strategy, the student will be on to the second. Teach this student to sound out the first part of the word, go back and read the line again with the first part, and add the next sound. Say a sentence reads *The mouse ran across the carpet.* The child stops at *carpet*; uses the first strategy to no avail; uses the second strategy and gets *car* — encourage the child to read the sentence again and then say "car-p-..." The word will probably come out like magic — and he'll say "carpet."

- Some students reverse words such as *was* and *saw*. Continue to do the transfer for them every time you come across these words and continue to have them track print with a finger. Here is something you can try for students who know all the strategies and are already transferring many words to text. When they mix up *saw* and *was*, look at the words on a separate piece of paper where you have printed the two words. Together look at what makes them similar and what makes them different. Students learn early on that print is tracked from left to right. For kids who continually reverse words, teach them to do the one-to-one match by placing their finger under the first letter of the word (as opposed to the middle of the word as is usually done). As they read these words in text they begin to use their finger as a tool. If *s* comes first, they know the word is *saw*; if *w* comes first, they know it's *was*. This little "trick" is simple to do and it really works well.

- Some other words, such as *took*, may pose difficulties too. Again, have the child try all strategies and use this fine-tuning tip only when the child is able to execute the strategies and is transferring words to text. If, after trying the strategies, the student is still unsuccessful, read the word for the student and say, "It looks like the word *look*, so it probably rhymes. Let's try it." You can write the two words on a piece of paper and say the two words as you point. Try other rhyming words to ensure the child is familiar with rhyming. If the child has difficulty with rhyming, fine-tune your instruction again and spend a bit of time on simple rhyming words.

- Some students will take some time to really flourish. Work with these students as often as you can. I had a Grade 3 student who was learning English as a second language. He could chant the first four columns of the high-frequency word list but was transferring few words to text, even though I was doing the transfer for him often. While the transfer to text usually takes months, he was taking an unusually long time. I kept the chant going — all four columns — and adding one word a day as usual with the class. During one-on-one instruction, I would have him chant and point to the Level 1 words, concentrating on just the Level 1 column. I told him to look closely as he read them and slowed him down a bit. When he read leveled text, I was sure to do the transfer every time we came across any of the words in the four columns. He eventually started to transfer the Level 1 words, and then we followed the same procedure for the Level 2 column. All students will read. If you follow the program closely, assess and analyze regularly, and make slight necessary changes, success will come.

As stated before, some children simply need to know what their job is in order to progress in reading. You have to tell them that reading needs to make sense. You have to explain what making sense means. You need to tell them that whatever they say has to match the print in the text. You need to tell them that it is their job to point to words as they read and be sure that it is correct. You need to tell them that, if they think they made an error, it's their job to go back and correct it. You need to explain to them what it is that they are doing that is causing the problem, and then tell them how to correct it. If a child doesn't know where the goalposts are, the child cannot score. We need to be sure that our students know exactly what is expected, what their job is as readers, and how to improve. It is remarkable how this explicit teaching can make a huge difference. I've met some children who knew their letter sounds and high-frequency words, and could sound out words with ease — but couldn't read well. When I did an Observation Record, they made several errors. Sometimes the errors still made sense and sometimes they didn't. They often inserted words and omitted others. They were children who did not know their job. I told them it was their job to make sure that everything they say matches the text. I also relayed that, if the reading doesn't make sense, it was their job to go back and fix it. I encouraged them to use their finger and point to each word, thus slowing them down and forcing them to attend to the print. They were able to read the text with much accuracy after that.

It is likely that you will feel like you have a student who will never learn to read. To feel this way is normal. The reality is that some students will take a much longer time. Does this mean the student cannot learn? What we need to do is to counteract beliefs about innate intelligence and how it affects ability to learn. My big struggler was identified as a student with multiple learning problems. By the time he had reached Grade 4, he did not know one letter sound and could not read one word. He had been through lots of remediation and the resource teacher worked with him daily. For a while, I was convinced that this child would be the one that wouldn't be able to do it. He was so far behind. I knew what he couldn't do, but was not looking for what he could do. I reflected and realized that I needed to change the messages I was sending — I needed to believe he could learn to read. We worked together for five minutes a day (if I found extra time in a day, he would get it). From the first day, he felt like a reader. He started to make progress — it was slow, but it was happening. It took well over a year, but he started reading books at grade level. At no point should we say that a child will never learn to read. We may say the learning may take a while, but as long as we can find five minutes in a day, success will come.

Telling students what their job is clarifies expectations, increases their understanding, and encourages the teacher to stay out of it!

Teachers are inherently helpful people. They want to do a great job and provide assistance to their students. They point for their students, tell them when they've made an error, and even turn the page for them. It is important to teach the child to be as independent as possible. Sit on your hands if you have to!! Let them point, turn pages, and point to the words. Give them room and time to discover the reading process.

According to Daniel Willingham, "Americans, like other Westerners, tend to view intelligence as a fixed attribute, like eye color. If you win the genetic lottery, you're smart, but if you lose, you're not." Some cultures see intelligence as more malleable, believing that "intelligence can be changed through sustained hard work" (*American Educator*, Spring 2009).

Students who are slower to accelerate can use as much one-on-one instruction as you can provide. This extra time will make a big difference. Any time that you can find to work on an individual basis with your students will accelerate the process. Hearing and seeing the high-frequency words over and over again has worked to help all students retain these words. If they need to see it a 1000 times, show it to them 1000 times. Some students need repeated exposure to letter sounds and words. This does not mean that something is wrong with them. What is does mean is that they can learn and will learn. We often equate not understanding at first to not being able to learn. This simply is not true. When we look at other countries and the success they've had with education, it is work ethic and motivation that are highlighted. Effort as opposed to ability is the key to success.

All students need to be praised and encouraged for every small step. Even if the progress is slower for some, they will get it and will start to read. Remembering the child's struggle helps us to be patient. Be positive, and then be more positive. Every success, no matter how small, must be celebrated. Try to remember that it is really hard work for a child who struggles to read. The progress that the child is making is remarkable even though it may not be at the pace we would like.

Making Use of All Resources

The Resource Teacher

The resource teacher has the advantage of working with few distractions, working with small groups or providing one-on-one instruction. In close communication with the classroom teacher, the resource teacher provides extra support for the students who are behind. The classroom and resource teachers need to discuss their observations. It is a good idea to take turns observing each other while you work with struggling students. Someone observing you teach can help you by watching to be sure your words and actions convey your belief in the child.

Using the diagnostic information the classroom teacher has gathered, the classroom and resource teachers will be able to determine who needs extra practice. From there, decide which students from the class can be grouped together, who requires the one-on-one instruction the most, and how the timetable will be best scheduled.

Here are some tips for resource teachers using the 3 Habits:

- As a resource teacher, you may be working with all the struggling students in the building, so how do you keep track of it all? Use the Reading Level Tracking Sheet (page 52), which allows you to track the levels students are at.

- Look at the number of students in each class who require extra assistance. Group students according to book level and work with small groups. If a student is progressing really slowly, working with this child on his or her own will garner the best results. Working with older students individually (Grade 4 and higher) also seems to be the best arrangement, so the student is not worried about others knowing about his or her current reading situation.

- Follow the same sequence as the classroom teacher. Teach all components each day. Work on individual letter sounds if required, then the combinations. Post the high-frequency words on chart paper and have a copy of all the words for each child in a duotang. You might wonder if you have to note which word the child last worked on, as you might not get to that child again for a couple of days and won't know where to begin next. This is not necessary and just becomes extra paper work in an already busy day. The child will chant as far as he or she can, and that will be your guide. Once students get used to the program, they will tell you what column they are working on. Tracking of the words is not necessary.

- It is the same for the individual letter sounds and combinations. See how far the child can chant, and then add one a day.

- You have the advantage of spending extra time on the reading of the leveled book. You can complete more Reading Checks and can listen to the child read the whole book. Extra time spent on this component is time well-spent. Once you become familiar with the program and the assessments, completing a Reading Check for all students who receive one-on-one instruction every day will not be too much. This does not mean students will read an entire book. Having students read a few pages to allow you to see exactly what they are doing and how to guide them will pay dividends. Analyze the Reading Check, share it with the classroom teacher, and look at the assessments you have both completed. Is the child ready to be bumped up to the next reading level? What is the next small step?

Given your experience and the fact that you were selected to work with students who lag behind, you probably are quite patient. As you know, some days students may not perform as well as they are able. They are like us — if we were to learn a second language, we may be really "on" one day, and not so sharp the next. The change in day-to-day performance is normal. Reading is a very complex task and can be extremely difficult for some. If you keep to the 3 Habits, the child will feel successful at every lesson.

Home Support

Teaching children begins at home well before a child reaches school-age. When the child begins school, the reins are not (or should not) be passed over to the teacher. It is a partnership — the parents and teacher work together in order to create the optimal conditions for the child's success. How does a parent help at home if there is no regular communication taking place? The best advice for teachers is to involve parents as much as possible. Most parents want to know how to help at home.

When you begin implementing the 3 Habits and the reading program, parents of your struggling students need to be trained as to how to offer support at home. They need to know that believing in their child and motivating her or him is key. They need to understand that flashcards are not part of the learning, and that the memorization is crucial.

Parents will need materials at home. The teacher has a set of duotangs with all necessary materials — enough for each student in the guided-reading group and one handy at the teacher's desk for quick assessments and lessons. Another duotang is in each struggling reader's desk for independent practice. A duotang with the letter sounds, high-frequency words, and reading strategies will need to go home as well.

Students take home a book each night to practice at their instructional level. Many schools have leveled take-home books that are easily accessible to students, and a system in place that causes little work for the teacher. It is a good idea to have books at grade level within each classroom, sorted into a basket for each reading level. Each day the child takes the book from a plastic resealable bag and switches it for a new one. Once students get used to the routine, it goes very smoothly. If the child returns a book, a new one can be selected. Tracking of books going to and from home is not necessary. Students can choose books from the correct leveled basket during silent reading time. During this time, the teacher may be able to complete some Reading Checks (a few each day) to be sure all students are at their instructional level.

How do we communicate information effectively to our parents?

Newsletter

When the 3 Habits are implemented schoolwide, information is communicated through the school newsletter. See page 72 for a sample insert for the newsletter.

Literacy Night

Many schools have what is called a Literacy Night, when parents are welcomed in to learn about all aspects of the comprehensive literacy program at school and about how they can help at home. I like to have the Literacy Night in the fall, once the reading program is underway and we are ready to send the newsletter item and the duotang of materials home. Parents are walked through a typical literacy block. We discuss the 3 Habits and how we weave them into the day. We explain how it is part of the learning-to-read program from Junior Kindergarten to Grade 1, and how it works as an intervention from Grades 2 and up. We explain that all kids can learn and that there are different ways to learn the same material. We relay our belief in our students' abilities.

We let parents know how they can help at home.

- We explain the chanting of letter sounds and high-frequency words, and the reading strategies.

- We show them the duotang that will be coming home and its contents (letters, words, and strategies) and we project these sheets onto the screen.

- When the letters are displayed on the projection screen, we show the parents how to chant them. We tell them that, when the individual letter sounds are mastered, another sheet (combinations) will come home and this will be chanted instead.

- We display the words on the screen and demonstrate how to chant. We explain how we chant in class and tell parents to start at the beginning (Level 1) and add one word a night.

- We make clear that the memorization is the route to success and that they are to refer to the memorization as "reading."

- We talk to the parents about motivation and empowerment. We tell them that, as their child gets used to the program, the child will be able to articulate which column to work on.

Have a literacy night as soon as you start using the program (even if it is the month of May). I always contact the parents or guardians regardless of the time of year so that they are doing it at home too. You will find students progressing from the start as they feel like readers.

- We let parents know that we regularly assess students and how a leveled book will come home daily that is not too hard or too easy (instructional level).

- We show the parents how to do the transfer of words.

- We display the reading strategies and tell them that, when their child is stuck on a word that is not on the Power Words list, this is what we use and what should be used at home.

- We explain how they can do all of this, how it will only take five minutes, and what a big difference it will make.

As principal of the school, I would call parents of children who would especially benefit. I would tell these parents how impressed we were with the progress their child was making. I would explain that we were having a schoolwide Literacy Night and we would be talking about a program that addresses the need to get all students reading. I explained how their attendance would especially benefit their child and would help their child advance at a quicker pace.

Incorporating the 3 Habits into the Literacy Night works well, as you will reach all parents. You do not want to advertise the night as being for families with struggling students, as there is a negative connotation and attendance will be low. You will be more likely to get more parents to attend when they see that the evening is for everyone.

As the classroom teacher, you may want to meet with your parents individually after the Literacy Night. If you have parents who do not attend the Literacy Night, you will certainly want to contact them and set up an appointment.

I truly believe that all parents want to help their children. However, there are some parents who are unable to help themselves, parents who face such challenges that they are not actively involved in their child's school life. Can the children of these parents succeed? Absolutely. The child needs only you, the teacher, to believe in him or her — so plan your time and teach that child to read. The help from home will make the process go faster, but it does not determine the child's reading success.

There are also parents who are not confident in their own abilities, or have such terrible memories of school that they do not get involved. When these parents see the progress their kids are making and get positive feedback from you, they start to feel better about school and often start to help out at home. Encourage these parents to get involved and attend school functions by calling home with good messages and updating parents about their child's wonderful progress.

I talked to a parent who shared that he had not had positive experiences in school as a child. When his son began school, the phone calls soon started and notes were sent home. His son was not learning the material. He was having problems. Behavior was starting to become an issue. The parent started to dread the calls from school because he knew what would be said. He had no interest in attending school events. By the time his son was in the middle of Grade 1, the 3 Habits had been implemented. The parent was surprised and relieved to receive a positive phone call. By the end of the year, his son was reading above grade level. The father attended the next Literacy Night and shared with the principal that he wished had had the same experience when he was young, as he had always struggled. Another parent shared that they turned off the television in the evenings and instead read books together. As a school, we need to give others hope and not allow our kids to slip through the cracks.

Letter Home

If you are implementing the 3 Habits in a classroom or two and it is not schoolwide yet, send a letter home outlining the program. You can use the Newsletter item on page 72, which can be modified to act as a letter home.

Parent and Community Volunteers

How fortunate we are when parent or community members offer to volunteer in the school. Extra adults in the building make a huge difference and are too often under-used.

If a volunteer would like to help out in the classroom, use this valuable time in two ways. The first is to have the parent work with the class on an activity that it already underway to free you up to work with the lowest readers in the class. A good way to do this is to ask volunteers to come in when the students are able to work quite independently of you. The volunteer can help with the class for a short time while the teacher works one-on-one or with a small group at the reading table. You are the expert on your most struggling students and it is important that you work with these students as often as possible. This is the best way to utilize volunteers.

The other way is to have volunteers work with your struggling students. Volunteers must be properly trained first. Volunteers are sometimes used to do the chanting; extra review of the sounds and words really helps. They need to know how the list is expected to be memorized and how important it is to be positive. Give a duotang containing all the necessary materials to each volunteer. That way, they don't need to disrupt the class. They simply come in, tap the child on the shoulder to get his or her attention, and head to the reading table or hallway.

It is sometimes difficult for teachers to let their struggling students go with volunteers. Teachers sometimes feel that the students are out of the class too much and think it may be detrimental. Try to remember that learning to read is fundamental and your students are leaving the class for only a few minutes.

Reading Buddies

Many schools and classrooms are familiar with reading buddies. Older students from one class read with younger students from another class once or twice a cycle.

I have used reading buddies and have found it to be a great way to differentiate instruction. I would buddy up my students who were reading below level with responsible, enthusiastic students in older grades. Before the first session, I would spend time with the older students explaining the importance of offering praise and motivating others. I taught them how the components work. After that, my young students took over. They all knew what book level they were reading and they would access a book at their instructional level. Students working below grade level would take their duotang as well, and were ready to practice the letter sounds, high-frequency words, and reading strategies with their partners.

I make the session valuable for my At Level and Above Level students too. To start with, all students are accessing books at their instructional level. During the

Arrange to meet with the parents of all students working below grade level so they know exactly how to help at home.

Volunteers should not be asked to complete assessments. The teacher is responsible for completing diagnostic, formative, and summative assessments. Assessment is a chance for you to observe and analyze. It is a time for you to empower and set the stage for success.

guided-reading time that week, all students know what they are working on and are able to articulate this to their buddies. For example, they may be working on fluency, or on making relevant connections to their reading. You can circulate during this time to offer your assistance.

I suggest arranging another system with the teacher of these responsible older students. When the older student has a few minutes to spare (perhaps a test or assignment finished early), he or she comes to your class and works with a buddy in the hall, just to review the letter sounds and words. This will give your student the extra practice needed (on top of what you are providing) and will give the older student a wonderful leadership and volunteer opportunity. Since it only takes a couple of minutes, there is no downside to it.

We have started a new reading program this year based on 3 Habits. The program accelerates the reading process for all readers and helps students catch up to their peers. There are three components to the program:

1. High-frequency words
2. Letter sounds
3. Reading Strategies

We are sending home the Sight Word List, made up of words that your child needs to be able to read automatically. We do not sound these words out; they need to be seen as a picture. Have your child show you how we read the words in class. Find out which list your child is working on by listening to him/her recite the words in order. Have your child chant the list words in order every day. Please do not put these words on flashcards and do not test your child by putting the words in a different order. Add only one new word each day. Chant the words, with the new word added, with your child five times until he/she can chant up to that point independently. The chanting should take only a couple of minutes each night. Your child will be memorizing these words in order and that is what we want. Your child will soon begin to transfer these words to text very quickly. Using this chanting method really empowers students to feel like readers from the start and helps them to recognize these words quickly and easily.

You will also find a Letter Sounds sheet in this package. Have your child show you how they are chanted in the same order every day.

The leveled books are going home and students are making gains in their reading. Students are bringing home books that are at their instructional level. The instructional level is not too hard and not too easy, and should provide opportunity to practice strategies for unknown words. When your child is stuck, have him/her:

• say the first sound of the unknown word and reread, and then
• sound it out, then
• skip the word and come back to it.

Please return the book so your child may select a new one to bring home each day.

The JK/SK classes will receive only the Level 1 list (40 words) and the rest of the primary division will receive the entire list. As individual students in the JK/SK classes finish memorizing the Level 1 words, the whole list will be sent home for them too.

Should you have any questions or concerns, please do not hesitate to contact me.

5

The Habits by Grade

Beginning the 3 Habits early is a preventative measure. It ensures that students will not lag behind. When students lag behind for years, they become our at-risk students. They become at-risk for dropping out, being socially deviant, and not reaching their potential. To teach them to read after lagging behind for so long requires breaking of bad habits, boosting self-esteem, and dealing with behavior issues. It is, of course much better for the child (and the teacher) to not have the problem in the first place.

All students will be successful regardless of how late the 3 Habits begin, but it is best for all if it is started early. It is not about readiness for reading. It is about exposure to print and words as early as possible. At home, this starts at birth (sometimes even beforehand). At school, it needs to start in Junior Kindergarten. The 3 Habits start as soon as students begin school, regardless of background — language barriers, poverty, speech problems, or lack of family involvement. If we begin as soon as a child enters the school system, we reach the at-risk students before they begin to lag behind, before they begin to feel different and act out, and before they start to think and believe there's something wrong them.

It doesn't take long for children to realize that they are not progressing as well as everyone else. Beth was in Grade 2, and her desk was often parked outside the classroom. She was always misbehaving — and she had a very patient teacher. Beth was disruptive. She constantly spoke out of turn and argued, and could not get along with her peers. When students were working in groups, Beth worked alone, as no one wanted to be in a group with her. Why was Beth acting out? The answer was simple: she couldn't read very well and therefore everything was difficult for her. She was well aware that she was not reading at the same level as her peers. Her inability to read caused her great despair — after all, everything requires reading. She preferred to act out rather than draw attention to the fact that she could not read. Beth's teacher learned about the 3 Habits and began to instruct differently. Beth started to learn quickly. Her attitude toward school and her peers started to change. After some time, her desk was back in the classroom where it belonged. She was sitting in the class with her group. She didn't need to act out anymore. She could read!

When we think that certain students are too young, not ready, or not capable, remember that these are precisely the students for whom the 3 Habits are designed. These are the students who need it the most. On the other hand students are never too old to learn to read. These students lack the same components as younger students. They need to know their letter sounds, sight words, and strategies. Regardless of the grade you are teaching, if you have students who are reading below grade level, the 3 Habits will work.

Junior and Senior Kindergarten

In most Kindergarten classes, there is much diversity. The reading process began for some of your students well before you met them. They may have caregivers or parents reading to them on a daily basis, and this has been going on since birth. They know their letter sounds, can read some high-frequency words, and understand the one-to-one match of words.

Others in your class may have had few experiences with books and were rarely read to. These students are unfamiliar with print and may not know how to correctly orient a book. They have no concept that the print is read from left to right, and don't have the automatic return sweep. A few in your class may be learning English as a second language. Learning to speak the language is just commencing for them, and the reading process in their new tongue has not begun. Some may have speech language delays.

You sit back, look at your class list, and wonder how you are going to teach all these children who are at many different stages — teach them about print, letter sounds, high-frequency words, and how to put it all together to read.

Since most of your students will not know their letter sounds, high-frequency words, or reading strategies, the components are taught as a whole-class lesson (see the Rule of 5 on page 27). Then, during guided-reading time, differentiate your instruction to bring each child a step closer to independence. It is a good idea to try to do each of the components at the same time each day. Many teachers do the chanting of the letters and words first thing, once students are settled during circle time.

Some Kindergarten teachers have wondered if they should teach the letter sounds first, then, once the letter sounds are mastered, move on to the words. I have found an accelerated learning rate when teaching letter sounds, high-frequency words, and reading of text simultaneously. When babies are born, they are spoken to, sung to, read to — all at the same time. It just makes sense.

Letter Sounds

- Add one letter per week for this age group rather than one per day. The weekly letter sound seems to work best for the early years.

All letters and pictures can be enlarged and posted in the classroom.

- Enlarge and post the large *A, a — apple* card. The large cards are much easier for these youngsters to see and attend to. Take the time to decide where to post the card — not too high and apart from posters that can be distracting — being sure that all students can easily see it.

- Follow the same procedure as described in chapter 2. Will all students retain the sounds at this pace? Most will, but not all, but just keep going at this pace and the review, and it will come.

High-Frequency Words

- In Junior and Senior Kindergarten, the majority of your students will not know the words in the first column of the Power Words list, so begin working on the Level 1 list separate from the other columns.

- Write the first word on chart paper and use a pointer to point to the word.

- Follow the instructions in chapter 2.

What if you teach a split grade and your Kindergarten students know the Level 1 from the previous year? Your Senior students can go ahead at home and you can work with them during your small-group sessions at their level. Let the Seniors know that they are going to help the Juniors learn the words. Senior Kindergarten students love this. Their learning will continue with you in small groups and on an individualized basis. The whole-class session takes a minimal amount of time.

If a student does not have any concept of print and does not know letters, should that student be learning the high-frequency words? To answer this question we need to go back to the three things students need in order to read. They need their letter sounds, the high-frequency words, and strategies. Therefore, we teach them these three components regardless of where their starting point is. In fact, if they are behind their peers, they need as much exposure as possible. While doing all of this, we also teach all of our students how to become better at comprehending text.

• Add one word a day. The one-word-a-day pace works well at this level. Not all students will keep up to this pace, but don't leave the Level 1 list until all students are able to chant the words. Progress will be made if students are hearing the words chanted every day even if they are not ready to join in.

If you are teaching Junior Kindergarten and your students may be as young as three, you may have to work harder at getting them to focus visually. Seat students strategically and have the less-focused students up close to the chart in close proximity to you.

Send home just the Level 1 list (see page 22), separate from the other columns, to start, but not before parents/guardians know how to use it at home. See chapter 4 about home support.

Once the chanting is underway and the words and instructions are sent home, some students will race ahead of the others and the Level 1 column will be mastered. These are your students with well-developed visual memories. They remember the words with ease and are able to transfer the words to the text without a problem. With your careful observation and regular assessment, you will find which kids are ready for the entire high-frequency word list. Put the Power Words list in duotangs and have them ready for these students during your small-group time. Send the full 220-word list home for these kids to practice. Let the kids go at their own pace. They can handle the smaller print and their bank of high-frequency words will become massive. These students will need to know that you expect them to go ahead at home. Some students refuse to go past the word that the whole class is at, as they think they might disappoint the teacher!

How can you know what column these kids are on in the list and how to monitor it all? First, it's always done with the whole class each day, and you know to add just one word per day. In small groups and during one-on-one instruction, let the children chant down as far as they can. When the last voice dies out, add one word.

It is easy to get caught up in wanting the kids to really know (i.e., read) the words they are chanting. They will know these words eventually and will know them solidly — but the process needs to be followed. This process is the quickest way to get all your kids reading. Your highest-level group will go beyond where they would have, and your lowest-level group will not be left behind.

It is also tempting to post the next column of words (Level 2), as many of your students will be ready for this. The pace of this component is determined by the student that is the furthest behind. The words that the whole class is chanting do not change until every student has the words memorized in order. Since all of your students will be in guided-reading groups, you'll be able to differentiate your instruction based on student need; learning is not impeded for your stronger students and no one is left behind. The program fosters self-esteem and success, and this particular component allows children to feel that they are reading as well as everyone else when they can "read" the words with their peers.

When all students have mastered the Level 1 column, post the Level 2 column on chart paper, but leave the Level 1 list up too. Not only will it help all students read, but Kindergarten teachers have found the chanting of the high-frequency words really helps with writing. Students are able to easily find the word they wish to write by chanting down to it. They do not have to ask the teacher how to spell these words as they are able to find out for themselves.

By the end of the year, expect to get to the end of Level 1. Your students will be able to chant these 40 words without even looking. When this occurs, they have mastered the column. All they might know is the chant. They might not recognize these words in text, but we refer to the list as mastered. Of course, we want them to look at the words while they say them, but the chanting should be flawless. By the end of the school year, many of your students will be able to read these words in and out of context. A few of your students will know only a couple of words, but they are further ahead than they would otherwise be. They will need a bit more time. By the next year they will blossom.

Transfer of Words

Since you are implementing this component as whole-class instruction, it is a little different than described in chapter 2. The first day you are implementing the program, you have chanted the first letter sound and the first high-frequency word (i.e., "a"). Look for every opportunity to transfer the words. You will be teaching to the whole class (see the Rule of 5 on page 27), so start with a shared reading lesson.

- You are ready to read your book and, since your students have chanted the word "a," you will stop every time you encounter this word. Say, "We know this word." Go to the chart paper and point to the word; say, "Let's read it together." You and the kids will say "a." Go back to the book and say, "What's this word again?" Someone will shout out "a."

- As you add a word a day and chant these words, pay attention to what you are reading to the class and make sure you follow the steps and do the transfer correctly. The more you do this, the faster your students will be able to read these words embedded in text.

Small-Group Work

Guided reading is an important part of any comprehensive literacy program and it starts in Junior Kindergarten. Once your diagnostic testing is complete, all your students should be in guided reading groups according to their instructional book level.

When you bring any of your students together for a guided-reading session, it's a good idea to have the Level 1 column on a piece of chart paper where you and the kids can easily access it from your guided-reading area. Only the students working beyond Level 1 should have the Power Words list in a duotang, as the small print may be difficult for your other students.

In their guided-reading groups, students have the opportunity to practice the transfer of the words from the list to the text. The transfer is taught in the same way as described in chapter 2.

There may be students who won't catch on to reading as quickly as others, but we know this doesn't mean they can't learn. It means that these students will need you to spend extra time with them.

Reading Strategies

- You will probably have a big book from which you are reading. Choose the book carefully, looking for books that lend themselves well to the first strategy, which is about meaning. These books will have pictures that match the text, and will enable you to model for students how we look at pictures and think about what makes sense.

- While reading, transfer words every chance you get, and model the first strategy. Imagine there is a picture of a cat and the text reads *A cat*. You transfer *A* for your students and then you point to the next word, *cat*. Say, "I'm not sure about this word." Take every opportunity to teach very explicitly to meaning. Say, "I'm going to help myself by saying the first sound and going back." Say, "A c___" while modeling the one-to-one match. Then say, "I wonder what this word can be. What would make sense? I'm going to see if the picture will help me." Discuss the picture with your students. Go back to the sentence and say, "A c__. Who can tell me what word would make sense here?" If no one volunteers, say, "Do you think it says 'A dog'? 'A horse'?" Someone will shout out, "A cat." Then say, "Yes, it does say 'A cat'," while pointing. "That makes sense."

- Finish reading the book, stopping a couple more times to get them to figure out the unknown word (just like you did with *cat*) by using meaning (*Say the first sound, and go back*).

- Since your students have chanted only "A, a, apple" so far, give the first sound of other words. If the unknown word starts with the short-a sound, look at the first letter of the unknown word and say, "We know this sound." Go to the posted card and say together, "A, a, apple."

- Always model the one-to-one match, which is one point for each word (not syllable). Say, "Look how I point to each word." Since you have students who probably do not know the difference between a letter and a word, you want to demonstrate the difference between words and letters as you come across them in reading.

With all your great modeling, you want students to equate the first strategy of "Say the first sound, and go back" with meaning, as you teach them to pull it from the text and pictures. You will keep modeling just this first strategy until your class understands it and is able to do it independently. Most of the year will be spent on the first strategy. The second strategy (*Sound it out*) is not modeled in front of the whole class until your students are ready for it. The second strategy can be taught in guided-reading sessions to students who are able to execute the first strategy independently.

If most of your students are ready for whole-class modeling of the second strategy (*Sound it out*), begin with the first strategy and stress that the strategies are always done in this order. You'll most likely still have a group of students who are working on the first strategy, so they'll keep working at that one.

Small-Group Work

Most students enter Junior Kindergarten unable to read a Level A or Level 1 book independently. Not only should guided reading be occurring, but your weakest students should have a daily session. This is where they learn how print works, how to point to each word, look at pictures, etc. If the child is unable to do the one-to-one match, guide his or her finger and help the child point. These students still receive all components of the program. They may not be able to use all components at this point, but they need the repetition.

A guided-reading session at the beginning stages would be about pointing to each word as you read it. When you get to a word that they chant as a class, do the transfer. Say, "You know this word" and so on, just as described in chapter 2. Your students may not be able to point to each word, but still do the one-to-one match with them, review the letter sounds that you have covered, and always do the transfer. As they start to figure out the patterns in early readers, they will take on more responsibility as readers. They will point and use the pictures. They have experience with the first strategy from your whole-class modeling. Once the one-to-one match is underway, you introduce the first strategy in your small-group session by saying the first sound for them and talking about what word would fit.

Many of your students will just be starting to use the first strategy independently when they get stuck on an unfamiliar word. This is excellent progress. The child now has one very good strategy to use for unknown words.

The key to success is to be reflective. Think about your kids. Assess your students often. Are they ready to move up? What instruction do they need in order to advance? Think of the peoplepower in your building. Can older kids help out? Do you have volunteers who can provide extra practice for your most struggling readers? Remember that your most struggling students need you. Plan for five minutes each day.

Grade 1

Most students come into Grade 1 having attended Kindergarten, so they will know the letter sounds and some high-frequency words, and will be able to read early readers. A few of your students will be reading at a mid-Grade 1 level and beyond. You may have three or four students you are concerned about as they lag behind their peers.

Look at your class list and start your diagnostic assessments. Use the Rule of 5 (see page 27) to determine if you will deliver instruction to the whole class as well as to small groups, or just to small groups.

Letter Sounds

Most of your students will probably know the letter sounds; but every class is different, so use the Rule of 5 (page 27). If you have more than five students who do not know the letter sounds, start with the letter sounds. If not, start with the combinations; in Grade 1, most students will need to learn the letter combinations, so teach them to the whole class.

If more than five students will benefit, enlarge and post cards for the combinations, beginning with *sh*. Introduce the letter combinations by saying, "Certain letters stay together when we read. When we see *s* and *h*, we say 'sh' like in the word *she*." After that, start the chant: say "sh" three times together and have the students say it once independently as described in chapter 2.

Once students begin chanting the combinations, the second strategy (*Sound it out*) may need to be modified. It changes to *Look at what needs to stay together, then sound it out.* We want students to really look for the digraphs and blends embedded in the text. If the letter Combinations sheet (page 31) is kept handy, the child can chant to the sound needed and then go back to the word to successfully sound it out.

High-Frequency Words

Start with the column required for your most struggling student — most likely the Level 1 words. Put the column on chart paper and post where all students can easily see it. Most students in Grade 1 are able to chant the first three columns of the high-frequency word list by the end of the year.

Follow all instructions from chapter 2. Stick with the Level 1 list until all students have memorized it perfectly and without hesitation.

You might wonder if your students need to be able to read these words before moving on to the next column. They need only to be able to chant them in order before proceeding. We encourage the kids to point to the words on the list so they attend visually.

Again you might wonder, when all your students are ready to start the next column except for one, if would it be wise to go ahead. I wouldn't even talk about the next list unless all students are ready for it. Remember that the program is for the most struggling students. Give these students extra time every day — as much as you can. Get older students, parent volunteers, and families working with them; five minutes at a time will get them going. Your other students can work on the lists and go ahead at home, and you can talk to parents or write a note home about this. But don't discuss the progress of others in front of the class. Go ahead on your list in your guided-reading groups, and praise the advancing students when you conference with them. We want the struggling students to feel as though they are doing what everyone is doing.

Study your students carefully and get to know them well. Observe carefully when students are chanting the list. Who needs extra help and a couple of extra minutes per day? Start planning for your guided-reading sessions. Once you have begun the program and your diagnostic assessments are completed, guided groups should begin — the quicker, the better.

Reading Leveled Text

Grade 1 is a time of tremendous growth in reading. The early years build the foundation and most students are just beginning to get the hang of the concept of reading as they enter the first grade. Students are expected to go up several levels in reading by the time they finish Grade 1. The guided reading and one-on-one time will be invaluable to you for observation. The wise reading teacher is carefully observing and noting the next small step for each student. The wise reading teacher is assessing regularly, and is sure all students are at their instructional level in order for them to practice their strategies and be successful.

"Modeling should be short and sweet…[we] then quickly engage kids in guided practice. Most of our instructional time is spent in guided practice because that is where we can best support kids as they move towards independence." (Harvey and Goudvis, 2007: 33)

Grades 2 and 3

You have a vast range of reading ability in your class. Some students are well above grade level and are reading chapter books. The majority are at grade level.

A handful of students are unable to read text at grade level — this is the group that the 3 Habits will benefit the most.

By this time, students who lag are acutely aware of it. They come in with the weight of the world on their shoulders. There are often behavior problems surfacing. They dislike school and the last thing they want to do is read.

A note to teachers teaching Grades 2 and 3: the 3 Habits make up a learning-to-read program. Since many of your students will come in as readers, they will not need all parts of the program. The chanting of the high-frequency words as a whole class is still essential for your struggling readers, even if you have only one student who struggles. But the other parts of the program are designed to be used in small groups or one-on-one for only the struggling students in these grades. Any student not at grade level will need all the components every day.

Letter Sounds

Students who are not reading at grade level may or may not know all of their letter sounds. These students will need to be tested by you on a one-on-one basis. These students have had much time to work on letter sounds in Kindergarten and Grade 1. If they still don't know their letter sounds, it's time to zone in on what sounds are lacking and tackle them. It is rarely all the sounds they don't know by this age; it is usually the vowel sounds and a couple of consonants. You will know exactly where to start from the diagnostic assessments you have completed.

Once you know which letter sounds are not solid, work on these sounds each day. Remember to work on the short vowel sounds, and the hard *g* and *c*. If the child only needs *u* and *w*, just work on these sounds using the Letter Sounds sheet (page 30). Go over the two sounds in the same order each day.

When your struggling students know the letter sounds, move on to the combinations. Provide a reading duotang for each student for all their materials.

High-Frequency Words

Grade-2 and -3 teachers will need to determine the starting list for the high-frequency words for their particular group of students. Have your most struggling student recite the Power Words list starting with Level 1. Always gear the column you will be working on to your lowest-level student.

Organize your day/week so you are sure to have time to work in small groups. That will ensure that everyone is working at their instructional level and on the list words they are currently mastering.

If a child is not able to easily and fluently recite the words in a column, this is the column you will work on and chant with the whole class. If the child can read most of the words but is stuck on a couple, this is still the column you start with. Remember that we don't want anyone to know that we are working on this list to benefit the struggling readers. The class will chant the words and won't be aware of the fact that it is for a select few. The procedure is the same as described in chapter 2.

Your most struggling may know the Level 1 words but not the Level 2. Record the Level 2 words on chart paper. Introduce nonchalantly, saying "We are going to read these words together." Prepare to hear, "We already know these words." Matter-of-factly say, "That's great — so here we go."

There may be Grade 2 and 3 classes (i.e., with a large ESL population) that have a large number of students working below level, therefore the Rule of 5 (see page 27) might apply.

Since the below-level students know they are lagging behind, it is imperative to work with them in such a way as to not highlight the basic level of the material. These students may be embarrassed that they don't know their sounds yet and don't need any more hampering of their self-esteem.

As a class, you should be working on only one new column. Even if you are teaching a split grade, the lowest-level student guides you, and you use that one column.

Send the Power Words list (pages 20–21) home with your students who need extra practice. Students are often so empowered they become self-motivated and read the list whenever they get a chance — they enjoy practicing at home. Even the ones who lack home support practice at home on their own! I've found that even parents who have a history of not working with their kids at home get caught up in the excitement, and begin to work with their kids.

Reading Strategies

As you know, most struggling readers will do one of two things when they are stuck on a word. They will either freeze or guess — and by now these have become well-ingrained habits. You have to work hard to break them.

Be very explicit. Tell the child exactly what he or she does at difficulty. Say, "When you're stuck, you freeze or guess, and these two things don't help you. Instead, this is what we're going to do. Every time you get to a word you don't know, I want you to say the first sound, and go back and read the sentence again." Have the student do this every single time he or she is stuck — it will help the student only some of the time, but at least this student has one useful strategy to use at difficulty. When the child attempts the strategy and the strategy does not help solve the word, model the second strategy and solve the word for the child. Don't teach the second strategy until the first is mastered.

Students that are below grade level in reading will have a small-group session every day. These students can use as much time as you can give them; if you can arrange a one-on-one session, do so. You may have time to listen to the child read only a couple of pages, but it will be worth it.

Every day, organize your day in order to deliver the reading components. For five minutes a day, chant the letter sounds, chant the high-frequency words, and read.

Older Students

Teachers who teach students beyond Grade 3 should deliver one-on-one instruction, rather than whole-class instruction, for all components, as self-esteem issues may come into play. However, if you have a high population of students who struggle or are ESL, and you don't feel self-esteem will be an issue, then whole-class instruction would be appropriate.

Students in the later grades who do not score well on Observation Records may have lots of skills — they may know their phonics and have a large bank of words. They may have some good reading strategies they use. The problem with some kids is that they don't track the print properly. These kids sometimes just need to be told exactly what they are doing. You might have students who insert and omit words frequently when reading aloud. Point this out to them in a supportive way and tell them that whatever they say has to match the print.

Other struggling students simply lack confidence in their ability and are unsure as to why you are listening to them read. Explain that you aren't interested in how they sound, or the speed at which they read (they often try to impress you by reading quickly); you are interested in listening to a story that makes sense. Explain to them what this means and give examples. This usually results in a better read, as they start paying attention to the message from the text and don't make careless errors.

Final Thoughts: Creating the Optimal Environment

It is well-known that when we are in an environment where we feel comfortable, appreciated, and safe, we thrive. If we know that our opinions matter, that we are listened to and valued, it's a place where we want to be. When we know what the expectations are and that much is expected of us, and we are given the tools, time, and guidance to reach our goals, we surpass what we think we're capable of.

Teachers have a tremendous responsibility. We are given the task and honor of working with our future. We take students, regardless of where they come from, and play a huge part in molding them into contributing and content citizens. Schools are so rich with ideas, values, and moral code that it's a place where many students find great solace.

In your own classroom, remind your students every day that you know they are smart, and that sometimes learning is hard work but that you're there for them. Do whatever it takes to reach your students. Try something new. Observe your students and see how they learn best.

Think of the classes in the school where all students are well-behaved. These students have had very clear expectations set for them, and the same has to be done for everything you do in the classroom. Students need to know exactly what you expect of them. When learning to read, students need to know what their job is, and that your expectation is that they will learn to read (and read well!).

For optimal student success schoolwide, the 3 Habits work best if the following is true:

- the principal supports the program
- the 3 Habits are used as part of the learn-to-read program from Junior Kindergarten to Grade 1
- all classroom teachers use the 3 Habits and deliver the reading components daily to all students working below level
- the resource teacher also delivers the reading components to the small groups or individuals furthest behind as often as possible
- trained volunteers/parents deliver some components of the program as often as possible

If you are the only teacher, or one of a few in your school, using the 3 Habits, your students will learn to read and will be successful. But when you are part of a team, with your colleagues and community all working toward the same goal as you, you will accomplish your goal faster.

When the 3 Habits are used, schools start to score well in all areas. Is this because all students are able to decode? This plays a part, but what is more important is that students are empowered; they believe in themselves.

What plays the biggest part of all when an entire school starts to move is the commitment from everyone. It begins with leadership — the principal. The principal must believe in students and this must be reiterated regularly. The principal must ensure that all students who are behind in reading are working with their teacher on a daily basis, and that the program is woven into the classroom schedule.

Teachers watch as students who had poor decoding skills are able to read accurately and fluently. If these students can learn to read, why can't they learn to infer, to make connections, to respond well to text, to write? These teachers experience the paradigm shift. Teachers continue to work with students in all areas. They analyze their data, work with students in small groups or one-on-one, and believe that each child will be able to improve. When teachers see the progress their students are making, they feel empowered that their hard work is paying off.

When the whole school works together and parents are seen as partners in education, the possibilities are endless. But this will not occur if the principal and teachers are not committed to student learning and do not believe that all students can succeed.

What does the commitment to reading success look like in the classroom? If a student is working below level in reading, the teacher assesses the child regularly through daily observations, completes formal assessments (at least weekly), and analyzes these assessments. The teacher is able to articulate exactly what the child's next step is. The teacher works with this child every day on all components. The teacher moves the student from small-group to one-on-one instruction if necessary.

If students know you believe in them and know exactly what their job is, and if you use the 3 Habits every day to teach them to read, they are going to rise to the occasion. If a student is not making the expected gains, that's okay. That student will get there. It may take all year, but that student will catch up. Stay focused on the progress the student is making.

To teach a child to read, especially one who has always struggled, is exceptionally rewarding. Ensuring that our students can read gives them all a fundamental start in life. Reading is about decoding and deriving meaning from text. The 3 Habits are all about learning how to decode and learning that reading is about meaning. The program focuses solely on these skills. A child will not be able to derive any meaning from any text if he or she is unable to decipher the code: the letter sounds and words, and how to read those words in sentences.

Keep your students reading at their instructional level. The books students read for guided reading, reading at home, and silent reading need to be at their instructional level. Students should be reading to you regularly at this level. They need opportunities to practice the reading strategies and to discover all they can about the reading process

While your struggling students are learning to decode, continue to teach them the critical literacy skills with the rest of your students, so they learn to derive deep meaning from text. Children who are behind in their decoding skills still need to be taught all aspects of your comprehensive literacy program. Do not move a child down in level if that child is not answering the questions that sometimes accompany the book. Children who are moved down in level will not be given the opportunity to improve their reading if they are not at their instructional level. Their poor performance in answering the questions indicates that they need support and practice working on this skill.

I don't think it is a question of whether a child is able to deeply comprehend text. The question really is this: are we spending the time to teach them how to express themselves and how to derive deep meaning from the text? If a student does not answer comprehension questions satisfactorily, it is an indication less of a lack of ability, and more of a lack of performance. Some students have speech difficulties and find it hard to express their thoughts. Other students lack confidence, especially if they have always lagged behind. It doesn't mean the thoughts aren't there. Teach your students that we read to get the author's message and to get information from text. Model strategies, have the child practice over and over again, and remind the students what their job is — to make sense of what they read.

Perhaps what needs to be stated is not just that every child can learn to read, but that every child can learn. We all need to be passionate about this and find ways to make it a reality.

Our students can learn anything, as long as we believe that they can and provide the support required. We need to keep working at unlocking the learning in all areas of the curriculum. If what you are doing isn't working, try something else. There's always a way to reach our students, we just have to find it.

Bibliography

Boushey, Gail and Joan Moser (2006) *The Daily Five*. Portland, ME: Stenhouse

Calkins, Lucy McCormick (2001) *The Art of Teaching Reading*. Portsmouth, NH: Heinemann

Clay, Marie M. (2001) *Change Over Time*. Portsmouth, NH: Heinemann

Covey, Steven (2004) *The 7 Habits of Highly Effective People*. New York, NY: Simon & Schuster

Diller, Debbie (2003) *Literacy Work Stations*. Portland, ME: Stenhouse

Fullan, Michael, Peter Hill and Carmel Crevola (2006) *Breakthrough*. Thousand Oaks, CA: Corwin Press

Gear, Adrienne (2006) *Reading Power*. Markham, ON: Pembroke

Gladwell, Malcolm (2005) *Blink: The power of thinking without thinking*. New York, NY: Little, Brown

Harvey, Stephanie and Anne Goudvis (2007) *Strategies that Work*. Portland, ME: Stenhouse

Harwayne, Shelley (2008) *Look Who's Learning to Read*. New York, NY: Scholastic

Kegan, Robert and Lisa Lahey (2001) *How the Way We Talk Can Change the Way We Work*. San Francisco, CA: John Wiley & Sons

Mighton, John (2008) *The End of Ignorance*. New York, NY: Random House

Miller, Debbie (2002) *Reading with Meaning*. Portland, ME: Stenhouse

Richardson, Joan (2009) "Looks Deceive" *Phi Delta Kappan*, June 2009; v. 90, no. 10: 698.

Routman, Regie (2002) *Reading Essentials*. Portsmouth, NH: Heinemann

Slavin, Robert, Gwen Carol Holmes and Cecelia Daniels (2008/2009) "Raising the Bar at Furness High" *Educational Leadership*, December 2008/January 2009; v. 66, no. 4

Stead, Tony (2009) *Good Choice*. Portland, ME: Stenhouse

Stiggins, Rick and Rick Dufour (2009) "Maximizing the Power of Formative Assessments" *Phi Delta Kappan*, May 2009; v. 90, no. 9: 640–644.

Willingham, Daniel (2009) "Can We Make School More Enjoyable – and Effective – for 'Slow' Students Too?" *American Educator*, Spring 2009; v. 33, no. 1: 10–11.

www.discovermagazine.com

www.marshallmemo.com

Acknowledgments

This book was made possible by support and encouragement from so many people. It began with a former principal, Terry Grand, who gave me the opportunity to learn about the reading process through the lens of Reading Recovery. I am grateful to all I worked with (teachers and students) and learned so much from, especially those from Hamilton with whom I trained and my Reading Recovery trainer Marsha Nesbitt.

When I developed the LIFE program (which is the basis for the 3 Habits) several years ago, my husband Anthony suggested I write it all down. I am thankful for his good advice and for picking up the slack (doing absolutely everything around the house) so I could have the time to write. I thank him for the countless hours he spent discussing the reading process and the unfolding of the book. He knows much more than he ever wanted to about teaching kids to read!

Thanks to Sue Boychuck. I am thankful to Sue for backing the idea from the start — her school was the first to field test my program. I am thankful to all staff members who worked so hard and volunteered their time. Thanks especially to Francesca Wood, Katie Bender, Branka Jones, Paula Schenk, Jane Ann Willick, Dani Chirico, and Jane Culp for the extra support and encouragement during the early stages.

I am so appreciative of all the support from the amazing school board I work for, District School Board of Niagara. Thanks to Barb McArthur for the opportunity. Thanks to Warren Hoshizaki and Carol Germyn for encouraging me and allowing me to present my ideas and program throughout the board. Thanks to Sue Greer and all the superintendents, principals, teachers, and educational assistants who supported me. I am so grateful to all who were willing to try something new, attend workshops, provide feedback, and allow me to visit classrooms and schools. I am deeply grateful. A special thanks to Ken Gennings, Cam Hathaway, Bev Smith, Gail Spear, Gary Osmond, Simon Hancox, Paula McIntee, Penny Fraser, Cindy Kohinski, and Jay MacJanet. Thanks to a great teacher and wonderful friend, Sue Keating (a.k.a. head cheerleader), who can talk about literacy all day long. She offered me great support, attended most (if not all) of my workshops (regardless of the weather), and promoted the program everywhere she went.

Taking my program to the next level of publishing would not have happened had I not had the good fortune to meet Lynn Taylor-Roehm, who has become a great friend. I hardly knew her at the time, yet she selflessly mentored, encouraged, and introduced me to the world of publishing. I cannot thank her enough for all she has done.

Having the book published was an incredible experience. I am so thankful to Mary Macchiusi for giving me this wonderful opportunity. I am lucky to have been given the chance to work with such a talented editor, Kat Mototsune, who transformed the manuscript with her keen sense for organization and detail.

Thanks to all those at Pembroke who worked behind the scenes, took the manuscript, dressed it up, and brought it into the sunshine.

Thanks to Kim Marshall. The Marshall Memo provided excellent summaries and quick access to professional articles, some of which I referenced to support the work in *The 3 Habits of Highly Successful Reading Teachers*.

Thanks so much to the countless volunteers with whom I have had the pleasure of working. Thanks especially to Nadine Furlong and my mother-in-law Jennie, who devoted several hours a week to read with kids.

I have deep gratitude for the endless support of family and friends (especially Fran Cerminara). Thanks to my dad for his enthusiasm, interest, and suggestions. Thanks to my daughter Madison, for her patience (as I monopolized most dinner conversations), for giving me time, and for turning down the music! Thanks to all my family and friends who encouraged me from the start.

Index